DISCARDIA

More Life, Less Stuff

DINAH SANDERS

Second printing, January, 2012.

Edited by Joanne Shwed, Backspace Ink
Cover design by B.J. West and Dinah Sanders
Book design by Joseph Gratz
Cover model Modesty B. Catt
Cover photograph by Reverend Dan Catt
Cataloging in publication by Rice Majors

This book is set in Hoefler Text, with headings in Verlag.

Sanders, Dinah.
Discardia : |b more life, less stuff / |c by Dinah Sanders ; edited by Joanne
Shwed ; cover design by B.J. West and Dinah Sanders ; book design by
Joseph Gratz ; cover photograph by Reverend Dan Catt.
p. digital, PDF file
ISBN 978-0-9839980-2-0 (trade paperback)
ISBN 978-0-9839980-1-3 (Kindle)
ISBN 978-0-9839980-0-6 (EPUB)
"Let go of everything that doesn't make your life awesome! With three key
principles and numerous practical tips, Discardia—a new holiday—helps
you solve specific issues, carve away the nonsense of physical objects,
habits, or emotional baggage, and uncover what brings you joy." - online
description
Contents: Three core principles -- March Discardia: Getting started --
June Discardia: Core principle #1: Decide and do -- September Discardia:
Core principle #2: Quality over quantity -- December Discardia: Core
principle #3: Perpetual upgrade -- Onward! -- Glossary -- Resources.
1. Success. 2. Motivation (Psychology) 3. Conduct of life. I. Title.
BF637.S4 S253 2011
158/.1--dc20

To parents, partners, friends, and teachers.

Thank you for loving me and helping me be a better person.

Contents

Part Four: December Discardia
Core Principle #3 — Perpetual Upgrade

Onward!

Glossary

Resources

Gratitude

Introduction

There is no need to hold on to what's obsolete: One
never loses what one tosses away deliberately.
—*Veronique Vienne, writer*

Living better through letting go

We are all busy people—busy with work and projects, busy with play and
dreams, busy with our communities and friends and families. We look
at our homes and think, "What a mess! There is no way I can get this
clutter under control without spending weeks working on it full time!"
We look at ourselves and think, "I'm a mess! What am I doing with my
life? What do I even *want* to be doing with my life?" It's easy to be overwhelmed by the seemingly vast distance between the way things are now
in our lives and the calm, clear lives we'd like to be enjoying.

We know we don't have everything we want. We know we have things
in our homes and minds that don't match the ideal we want for ourselves, but the idea of adding anything or taking on more to-do's to
change things is overwhelming. We view that dreamed-of excellent life
as a thing we need to squeeze into the overcrowded chaos of the one we
live now. The good news is that it's already in there, just buried and hidden under a bunch of stuff we don't need or want.

The quarterly celebration of Discardia—a new holiday—is the time
to carve away all the nonsense that isn't making us happy, and uncover
what does. We don't have too little; we've piled too much on top of ourselves. When we steadily scrape away the junk with one good decision at
a time, our true selves begin to shine through. Discardia doesn't require
us to change course radically; rather, it is the simple practice of leaning
the boat in the direction in which we want to sail. Little adjustments
lead us to wonderful new places.

Letting go and lightening our loads create positive motion; when combined with a light touch on the rudder—a little leaning of the boat—we have the ability to turn our lives in better directions.

The tips in this book, plus the supportive community of Discardia fans (whom, for convenience, I'll refer to as Discardians) found in multiple online locations, will help you put your energy where it counts: in making your dreams real and in living a less stressful life full of awesomeness.

So what, exactly, is Discardia?

It's a new holiday—invented by the author in 2002—with deep roots touching unconsumption, the slow movement, downshifting, and voluntary simplicity. Unlike many holidays, it doesn't involve obligations or expense or overblown expectations of specialness. It does not require us to interact with people with whom we do not wish to interact. In fact, it doesn't *require* us to do anything. Discardia is celebrated by letting go of what doesn't add value to your life—whether physical object, habit, or emotional baggage—and replacing it with what makes your world truer to your essential self. The core concept is this: If we continually discard what doesn't help us, we'll be left with more of what does—more space, energy, and time to make our lives even better.

Such a positive shift doesn't require taking a vow of poverty or scarcity but instead simply increasing the frequency with which we make choices that improve the quality of our lives. This transformation isn't a magical change that will happen when the stars align or some hundredth monkey does the right thing. It's practical and, for the majority of folks, it's not even that hard. (Note: If you're wrestling with a very serious challenge that moves you from the realm of clutter into hoarding, I recommend that you consider Discardia one of the other tools in your toolbox as you work with an experienced professional in that area. The International OCD Foundation and Children of Hoarders are good places to find more information and assistance.)

Discardia reminds us to think about what could we be doing or feeling if all this stuff wasn't in the way. It also reminds us to spend some time shifting our lives toward more of what makes us thrive. Each of us has a different definition of what that exciting, fulfilling, less-stressed life consists of, but the path we take to make it real is one we can travel together. Our first step is to remind each other to think about what we want and compare that to what fills our lives now.

Whatever enters our lives might clutter it up. We have a choice about letting it enter and about letting it stay. Our choices make us who we are. If we are aware of who we want to be, we can make the decisions that steer us toward our better selves and away from things that bog us down.

A guide to this guide

This book provides a practical introduction to the celebration of Discardia. We'll take a tour through the Discardian seasons with straightforward tips reflecting three key principles for building a happier life. Along the way, we'll hear how Discardians around the world have changed their lives for the better.

Though the book is arranged around a Discardian year, I recommend reading it straight through the first time no matter what season it is when you first celebrate Discardia. Most of the tips aren't bound tightly to the calendar and build upon one another. With the underlying principles under your belt, you can then dive into the appropriate section as reminders for future Discardia holidays.

You will also find an extensive list of resources at the end of the book, which you can use to dig deeper into some of the tools and techniques shared here.

———

This is not just another "throw out your crap" book. Discardia is a reminder and a framework for personal change. I want to give you the tools you can use to achieve a life that is ideal for you. Try them. Take the ones that work for you. Incorporate into this framework other good advice and techniques you've learned for simplifying your days, uncluttering your head and home, upgrading your life, and being true to your real self. Build the system that works for you from the good tools and techniques you find.

On any given day, work from the side for which you have the most energy by adding more access to what you love or carving down to less of what you hate to have in your way. You will find that a particular technique may be valuable to different people for different reasons. For example, you may be chatting with a friend and saying that you're going to spend the next 45 minutes working hard through your to-do lists—ready, set, go! This may work for one of you because of the synergy that comes from being connected and supported; for the other, it may work because you're less likely to procrastinate if you know that someone is paying attention.

Discardia is fun and flexible. Because the length of the holiday varies slightly on each of its appearances, it remains new and energizing, able to reflect the different rhythms of our lives. Enjoy yourself! It shouldn't just feel like you're flossing your apartment. Moving on from who you've been to who you're being deserves celebration.

When is it?

Discardia takes place four times a year. Sometimes it's short and sometimes it's long, since, in an effort to uncouple the holiday from any cultural bias, it is scientifically timed by our world's natural motions through the solstices, equinoxes, and their following new moons. The precise dates can vary depending where on Earth you're located, but I encourage you to discard being too fussy about that. Use the indicators in your own calendar or the dates I list on the Discardia website or just celebrate it sometime during March, June, September, and December each year. For convenience, the dates for the next few years (with thanks to the calculations of Discardian engineer Seth Golub) are:

- December 21–24, 2011

- March 19–22, 2012

- June 20—July 18, 2012

- September 22—October 15, 2012

- December 21, 2012—January 11, 2013

- March 20—April 10, 2013

- June 20 — July 8, 2013
- September 22 — October 4, 2013
- December 21, 2013 — January 1, 2014

There is also a public Discardia iCal calendar available at Discardia.com.

The daily art of living a Discardian life year-round

Celebrating Discardia once will make your life better than it was the day before. Celebrating it four times a year, every year, will begin to have positive, long-term impacts on your happiness. That's plenty of benefit for very little effort! If you really want to start feeling the wind in your sails, though, try being a Discardian every week or, better yet, every day.

> Throughout the book, you'll find text displayed like this, which will highlight timely directions you'll use on a daily or weekly basis, such as best practices for starting your day at work.

Open your eyes to the blockades you've put between you in this moment and where — and who — you really want to be. When you see those barricades, knock them down. Build bridges to your creative, happy self. Quick fixes can add up to deep changes.

I have been living the Discardian life for nearly a decade now and it has brought me more delight, in more aspects of my life — from the mundane to the most important — than I would ever have predicted. This approach to living has enhanced my work, whom I spend my time with, how I spend that time, and the myriad details of my daily surroundings. My enthusiasm for Discardia comes from knowing how much happier it has already made me and feeling the certainty that it can make us all — you and I — happier still.

In this book, I will share what I've learned in great detail, but I want to tell you something right now. Regarding the daily art of Discardia, there are two big habits you can use whenever you're faced with a choice or an opportunity:

- Continually opt for that which will most avoid hassles and unpleasantness in the long-term; and

- Continually make what you have to do more comfortable and enjoyable.

This is what makes the difference. Keep an eye out for a change you can make to improve things; then—here's the important bit—*do it*.

———

Can we have it all? All the good stuff and none of the bad stuff? Probably not, but if we have ever more of the good and ever less of the bad, that's a fine thing.

Three Core Principles

Core Principle #1: Decide and Do

> Making decisions requires energy, but not deciding
> about whether to decide requires even more energy.
> —*David Allen, productivity guru*

Celebrating Discardia begins with deciding what belongs in your life and what does not. Deciding now is the best habit you can teach yourself. Once you decide, you can act. Action changes your life for the better.

Without decisions, our lives become a constant accumulation of junk. Things pile up, usually literally. Magazines and newspapers, clothes with missing buttons, mail to read, half-finished projects, obsolete computer parts, and on and on. You know how to get rid of these things—trash, recycling and the Goodwill donation box—but the problem is making yourself get around to it. Rather than giving yourself a hard time, your first Discardian act should be to let go of feeling bad about what you haven't gotten done by now. You were doing something else; it was a choice; you're a big kid; it's okay.

Now that you've forgiven yourself, I'm not going to tell you to get cracking and change all your habits overnight. I am suggesting, though, that you start with a few small steps, which are the foundation for bigger changes. The key to fighting entropy is simple and threefold:

1. Slow down your accumulation of this stuff;

2. Make it easier on yourself to get rid of it on an ongoing basis; and

3. Habitually decide what you want to discard.

Act as your own gatekeeper and decide what gets in. As you control the inflow, increase the outflow to rid yourself of things that only serve to make your life more awkward and overstuffed. Ask yourself, "Why do I keep holding onto that?" and use your answer—or the fact that you have no answer—to decide whether it is time for that thing to leave. If this object or habit or emotion were only available by subscription, would you renew?

Make deciding as easy as you can. The more you do it, the easier it gets. You can even have a friend come over and help, holding up one object at a time as you lounge on the sofa with a glass of wine, giving them the thumbs up or thumbs down.

Part One, "March Discardia: Getting Started," will show you where to begin, and Part Two, "June Discardia: Core Principle #1—Decide and Do," will walk you through seven additional symptoms of indecision and their solutions.

Core Principle #2: Quality over Quantity

> My tidiness, and my untidiness, are full of regret
> and remorse and complex feelings.
> —*Natalia Ginzburg, author*

Paradoxically, the best way to feel like you have more is to get rid of things. Weeding out things that no longer need to be in your home—that juicer you never use, those books you'll never reread, that old beloved decorative item that has morphed somewhere along the way into merely an object to dust—can leave you uplifted and energized and draw your attention back to those things that do still matter to you.

It's not about denial; it's about being selective. When you've tuned your life to the point where it contains only what supports your goals, dreams, and values, you'll find what architect Sarah Susanka calls "a kind of moreness" that really makes you feel at home.

The same is true for the clutter in your head. Your time and attention are finite. Begin by letting go of self-pressure to do or think about more than is actually possible. Then, give yourself enough mental room to focus comfortably on what really matters to you. Allowing that space will optimize the effect of the time and attention you choose to apply. The true measure of success is to gauge your progress not by the number of actions or your busyness, but by the increasing closeness of your goals.

In Part Three, "September Discardia: Core Principle #2–Quality over Quantity," you'll make a shift toward a higher quality life through the solutions provided to 11 symptoms of quantity overload.

Core Principle #3: Perpetual Upgrade

Little actions add up to big changes.
—*Brad L. Graham, blogger and bon vivant*

Life is short; spend your money, time and energy where it enriches your soul. In every possible moment, lean toward experiencing the good stuff. Don't hesitate to optimize your world when it will save you unhappiness and not add to anyone else's. Note that getting a better version of something doesn't always mean spending a lot of money; you can find cheap or even free upgrades. When you've figured out something you need, it is the rightness of the solution–and not the price–that makes it work. For example, some of the most useful pieces of furniture in my home were free castoffs.

Strive to have ever better problems. Watch for the predictable roots to issues and continually hone your skills at solving, removing, or reducing their occurrence. When something feels wrong, trust your instincts and avoid it. Ask, "Am I getting what I need here?" Whether you call it perpetual upgrade, life hacking, or kaizen, keep tweaking your world incrementally in the direction of excellent.

Part Four, "December Discardia: Core Principle #3–Perpetual Upgrade," gives you 14 symptoms and solutions to instruct you in the art of fine-tuning your life.

———

As you work through the book, watch how something that is right (or close to right) can throw the wrong thing, the unneeded thing, or the outgrown thing into sharp relief. There is a tipping point of attention after which your surroundings begin to help you move in the direction you want to go. Your life lurches like a hot-air balloon filling up and, as you throw overboard the now clearly identifiable crap that isn't right for you, it starts to lift higher.

———

Whatever the reasons for having stuff you don't want or need crowding your life, the best gift you can give yourself is the ability to let things go. Make it your goal, as designer and social activist William Morris advised, to have nothing in your home that is not beautiful or useful—or both. Rid yourself of anything that does not make you feel more true to yourself. Small changes add up. At least during Discardia's four occasions a year, but ideally every day, take time to tune in and give your world a little twist toward the best day you can imagine.

Part One

March Discardia: Getting Started

Resolution review

Our Discardian year begins with the basics. When March rolls around, return to your foundations. Having survived another holiday season and done your big end-of-the-year thinking and goal setting, now is the time to look at the habits and ideas that have survived a few months.

- Which resolutions actually received your energy when the rubber hit the road?

- What goal still feels important but lacks the supporting structure for you to make it real?

- Where have you wandered off track or decided to change the route and what does that tell you about how your daily life can better support your vision for this year?

Give yourself a tune-up and make sure that the little stuff that you're adding up is working well to help you achieve a more fulfilling life.

Where to begin?

The biggest impediment to starting is the fear that you have to bite off a bigger chunk than you actually do. If all you do each time you start is move one thing closer to the way you want it to be, that is good. That is doing the right thing. Don't worry about finishing; just *start*.

Begin by seeing. Notice when you notice something that is either very wrong or very right in your life—and pay particular attention to what you do next after you have that realization. Does it help to decrease the wrongness and increase the rightness?

Getting depressed over something that's wrong doesn't help. Telling yourself, "This one right thing doesn't count because not everything is right," doesn't help. At minimum, acknowledge the observation, "This is not ideal" or "*That's* what I like!" The more you do this, the more you teach yourself to see your world. The more you see your world, the better prepared you are to make choices that will affect it. Those things that feel least like your ideal day can be a project for improvement, while those that are most like it can be a project for preservation and expansion.

Begin by relaxing. Changing things for the better does not have to be a battle. You do not need to take on your toughest challenges first thing. Quite the contrary, progress on the easy stuff will fuel your strength for bigger changes. You do not have to make every change perfectly. It's better to get moving in any direction—even the *wrong* one—and improve your trajectory as you go rather than stagnate and never start.

Begin by beginning. There is tremendous power in having a space where you can relax and not be crowded by random junk. That island of sanity can be your first goal and, soon, your touchstone for the kind of life you want to be living. Start your creation of this space in stillness at your favorite time of day. Turn off the TV and the radio. If you're at work, close the door to your office or put your chair—with a "BUSY!" sign on it—in the opening of your cubicle.

If you share your home, include the other residents in the project or get them out of your way. Set down whatever you're holding. Walk through your house or office looking not at the clutter but at the spaces, at the light. See through the contents to the place. Is there a view through a window that you particularly like? A special spot where the sunlight makes patterns and warmth? A quiet corner or a central place in the action that you love?

We're not talking about remodeling, so begin with the bones and breath of your existing space. Find the place that matters most or works best for you and begin with that. Getting the clutter and chaos out of your life is hard; you deserve a reward right up front. Having somewhere pleasing in which to sit and think is that first reward.

Now, if it makes you feel good and nurtured, get yourself something to drink—a cup of good tea, fresh juice, hot cocoa, a mug of coffee, or whatever pleases your senses of smell and taste—and put on some of your favorite music to please your ears.

Look at your chosen space. What is keeping you from enjoying it to the fullest right now? Maybe the right furniture isn't there. If it's going to be your reading nook and there's no chair and no good lamp and no handy spot to set down that cup of tea, that's got to change. If it's going to be your writing space and there's a TV or a file cabinet where your desk ought to be, that won't do at all. Maybe the furniture is there, but other furniture, knickknacks, magazines, and flotsam crowds it. In any case, some things almost certainly have to change. Begin with a few small steps and not necessarily by moving furniture. You might want to take a quick picture as reminder of your progress later.

Bring over a trash can and a recycling bin. Get yourself two boxes. Label the first box *Better Place*. Put in any items currently in your chosen space that belong somewhere else. Label the second box *Keep?* and place into this box anything you're not sure you want anymore. Make a quick sweep to eliminate things that don't belong here, discarding into trash and recycling or sorting into the two boxes as you go.

Remember: The goal is to clear your chosen space of anything that is not part of your vision for it. If you can't decide about something, put it in the *Keep?* box.

Move the *Better Place* and *Keep?* boxes to somewhere else in your house or stash them out of the way in your office. Unpacking them will be your next project after you have created your lovely chosen space.

Now look at your new territory again. Better, yes? Does it have the wrong furniture in it? This is the time when you could start rearranging your furniture but not before getting rid of the clutter. You see, if you get bogged down now, at least you got that junk out of the way and you've made some progress. Also, if you're moving furniture out— whether to another room or to storage or out to the curb—before you bring the proper furniture in, clean up your chosen space. Dust, sweep, wipe down. Make it uncluttered and fresh. If you don't have exactly the right piece of furniture yet, see if you have something close to serve as a placeholder for what you really want. Partway to your dream is still a good direction to be heading.

Say now, look at that—your space!

Enjoy it. Defend it against encroachment. Start your cleaning here so it's always the nicest spot. From this new castle you will plan your next campaign, or maybe just have the peace of mind to ignore the rest of the mess for a while.

Winning out against entropy

Now that you've got somewhere good to be, it's time to think about the best tricks for winning out against entropy (that is, the degree of disorder or uncertainty in a system). The first trick is that *easy is easy*; in other words, go for the low-hanging fruit, by all means! Two great examples of this are *big objects*, which have a more significant effect on you when they are very wrong or very right, and *categories* of things, which can be tackled en masse for a bigger impact. When faced with a huge number of things you could work on, try starting with one of these.

Categories are easier to handle than intermixed piles; you can set yourself up for easier starts in the future by chunking instead of randomly stacking. What's the difference between "stacks" and "chunks"? The items in a chunk represent the same kind of action. You'll get a very different feeling from four chunks that correspond to "phone calls to make," "vacation planning ideas," "clothes to exchange for correct size," and "scheduled events to add to the household calendar" than you do from one intermixed "stack of stuff I gotta do something about." Piles of the unknown create the most tension. Tackling a chunk is a lot easier because you know exactly how to start and understand the context of the work you'll be doing. Know what you have, then choose when to deal with the chunks according to your higher-level priorities.

Looking for the low-hanging fruit? Here are two examples to get you started:

1. Hall closet overstuffed and driving you crazy every time you try to hang up a coat? Pull out the one biggest thing in there that doesn't belong anymore and put it where it goes, whether that's somewhere else in the house or out of your life. Repeat this every time you notice the problem and before long the problem will go away.

2. Catalogs piling up on every flat surface? Throw them all in the recycling bin. Seriously. All of them. Worried there might be something you want in there and how will you ever know if you don't read it? Forget about it. If you need it, you'll seek it out. If you don't seek it out, you don't need it right now. It's easy to tell catalogs apart from other things; single-mindedly whipping through the house with the recycling bin, separating them from other papers, and purging all of them is a piece of cake. You'll be done in a few minutes! This kind of selective whirlwind works on other things, too, like dirty dishes and stale, old magazines.

Act on decisions as you make them

Another great trick for fighting the buildup of random junk is to act on decisions as you make them. One of the purest examples of this is to sort your incoming mail over the recycling bin. Don't think, "Huh, junk mail," and then set it down on the dining room table. Chuck it out right now! When you look at something and think, "I should donate that to Goodwill," pick it up *now* and put it in your charity box. Don't make yourself do the work of deciding more times than necessary. There are plenty of choices to make, so why add to that load with redundancy?

Ah, what was that about your charity box? This brings us to our first symptom and solution.

1

Clutter:
A Houseguest Who Won't Leave

Departing Now on All Tracks

> Through the years I have found it wonderful to
> acquire, but it is also wonderful to divest.
> It's rather like exhaling.
> —*Helen Hayes, actress*

> We cannot take our next breath without the exhale.
> —*Ellen Scott Grable, Discardian and artist*

Outbound trains

Stuff that doesn't belong in our homes anymore—or that never belonged there in the first place—has a tendency to pile up, stick around, and settle in with the intention of staying for years. Evicting that junk as soon as you recognize it for what it is will create space for positive change. Deciding that you want only things you care about in your home is a no-brainer; achieving that improvement is trickier.

We all prefer to do what is easy, so make it easy to do what you most want to have done. Grease the slope toward where you want to be. When the goal is getting stuff that doesn't make you happier out of your home, make outbound things obvious and easy to send on their way. Spatial convenience is your big ally here.

- Have a trash can in every room. They are magic. Fill it up today with things that are of no further use to anyone and put it out where the wizards will transform it into an empty one. *Abracadabra!*

- Have a recycling bin next to your desk and in the kitchen. Make it easy to purge yourself of dead paper.

- Get a shredder if you don't have access to one at the office or if you have a lot of things you need to shred at home.

- Always have an easily accessible and open charity box out of the line of sight where you relax. Whenever you come across something that's not trash, but you also know that you'll never really use it again, walk right over and put it in the charity box. Next time you're heading out for errands, grab that stuff and drop it off at Goodwill or wherever. (If you don't declare your charitable donations on your taxes, you don't need a receipt, so it takes almost no time to make your home nicer and someone else's life better. If you do declare donations, get some extra forms or use an online version to fill it out in advance for a faster drop-off.)

- Make a *Give Back* basket and put in it all the things that need to go back to the person from whom you borrowed them. You can also put outgoing gifts there. When someone visits or you're heading to their place, take a quick look in the basket for anything that needs to go to them.

- Find, buy, or make an aesthetically satisfying tray to act as your in-box for bills and receipts. Don't muddy it with nonfinancial stuff; get a separate inbox for that. (Tip: The *Bills* box is a great place for your postage stamps and envelopes to live.)

- You may find it handy to create a *Put Away* basket for each person in the house into which their stuff can be placed when left in a shared area like the dining table. When someone starts to ask, "Has anyone seen my ..." this is the first place they should look.

- If you use the library—and you should since it's free, after all— dedicate one spot for items ready to return to the library. A canvas bag on a shelf in the front hall is good and convenient for carrying any newly checked-out loot back home.

As Discardian Jason Eness put it, "What can't be sold can be given, what can't be given can be donated or recycled, and if it fails all that, I find a loving dumpster."

Routines help reduce stress

While you're thinking about a place for all these outbound items, take a moment to make your daily life easier. If you make a place for the things for which you know you'll need a place, you'll also reduce clutter.

- Choose a spot where your purse, briefcase, laptop bag, or backpack will go when you get home. Under or beside your desk is usually ideal. When you decide that you need to take something to work or school, put it there right away so it will go along for the ride.

- Decide where your keys live. Always put them there right away when you get home. Some people like a hook or a bowl by the door; others prefer a key clip in their purse or other constantly carried bag.

- Find a visually pleasing container to live on your dresser and throw your change in it at night when you empty your pockets while undressing. (Yes, I say always empty your pockets when undressing. Better to have clutter on your dresser top than wash that important business card or have to rummage through a pile of dirty clothes looking for your phone.)

- Use the front of your refrigerator (or a bulletin board beside it) for important household knowledge. Keep the tickets to the next event you're attending clipped there. If you share a house with a group, put up a rotating chore wheel to indicate who is doing what this week. This is probably also the best place for the shopping list and any menu plans for the week.

- Create a finite place for saving just enough and not too many bags for re-use. We have a *Bag of Bags* hanging in a closet (sung as though part of Handel's *Messiah*, of course) and if it's full, incoming bags are recycled.

Figure out what you need and where you'll use it, and then set things up to make it all flow smoothly.

Allow for just a little indecision

When you are uncluttering or sorting through old things, the key to a great session is to decide on sorting buckets before you start. In addition to having the usual outbound trains handy, allow some items to go into a *Not Sure* container. In a perfect world, every single thing is clear and unladen with emotional baggage, but I don't live there and I bet you don't either. Don't try to force an airtight system onto a far more complicated reality. Leave yourself a little slack. Keep moving on the easier choices to get your 90% progress while letting the 10% weird ones bide a little time to get less weird.

Combine trips

Here's a great lazy person's trick that is frequently mistaken for wild productivity. Don't make extra trips. When you're leaving the house, take a quick look for any outbound traffic that can come with you. Pop that stack of stamped mail in a postbox as you stroll. Swing by on your way to somewhere else and quickly dump your charity box in with the other donations or your library things down the book drop. Feeling especially sly? Train yourself that the way one does errands is to dump the trash and recycling, and then load the car and head out. You'll love the satisfaction of coming home from a run to the grocery store or an afternoon at the movies and finding your home pleasantly freed from that unwanted stuff.

————

Whatever else you do to make it easier for unwanted items to depart, find one thing in your home that makes you feel cruddy and get rid of it right now. One thing, *today*.

	SYMPTOM
2	## It's Hard to Start
	SOLUTION
	### *The Lap*

> We do not need the courage to write a whole novel.
> We need the courage only to write on the novel today.
> —*Julia Cameron, writer and artist*

Even a little is better than none at all

It can be difficult to get yourself in motion any day of the year, no matter who you are. When you first begin with Discardia, there sometimes comes a day when ya just don't wanna. So how do you fight this resistance to your life becoming more awesome? Well, it helps to remember that it's really what you're working on, but, even when we know we'll be happy about the outcome, it can be hard to start. The solution to this is to run *The Lap*. It takes many forms but, at its heart, *The Lap* is a deal with yourself to do a little bit *now*, instead of saying, "I'll do it later."

Any progress is better than no progress.

Jane Anne's one-room sweep

One very enthusiastic Discardian, Jane Anne Sorenson, takes a spatial approach by doing a sweep through one room. This technique (found in an article on Discardia at the goal-sharing website called 43 Things) is a great procrastination-buster. Jane Anne puts out three boxes—charity, recycle, and garbage—and sets a timer, moving clockwise around the room from the door, top to bottom. She makes a quick evaluation for each item, and it's either "love it," "need it," or "use it," in which case it stays where it is. If it's "don't need it," she puts it in a box.

This isn't about a one-time massive shift; what matters here is some stuff, which doesn't make the cut, goes away. Each time she runs one of her evaluation laps on a room, it moves closer to her ideal space. Her encouraging example is that powerful sweeps plus an overall vision plus just starting lead to success!

Go for the record

One of my favorite forms of *The Lap* is powered by something I love doing: hearing my favorite music. Listening to an album straight through doesn't take that long, particularly when you're doing something else, and good tunes can be a great motivator. Combine these two pieces of information and you're ready to go for the record. It will take less than an hour and your home will be much nicer afterwards.

Select an album. You will work steadily through the entire album, so make it a high-energy one on which you like all the songs. Avoid songs that make you cry, Gregorian chants, moody ballads, and New Age ambient space pudding.

Start the music and get through as much of your list as you can. Don't stop and do other things during the album and, when the album ends, don't stress over what remains. Things will be a lot more like how you want them to be; enjoy that and relax. Remember: *You aren't asking yourself to do the whole list right now. You're just doing the album.* You'll get as far as you get and that's fine.

The short lap

Sometimes a whole album's worth of plugging away takes more time or energy than you can muster. That's when a short lap is your best bet. Set a digital timer or put on some music and go for four or five songs. Don't say, "Later." Say, "__ minutes *now* and then I can stop." You'll be amazed at what a difference 15 or 20 minutes of focused progress can make against even the worst chore.

This approach can also train you to better define your tasks. When the very first step is obvious, the project won't repulse you as much. Strategic consultant Ethan Schoonover suggests writing to-do's as if you were delegating them to a real, other person. Be descriptive so your future self can leap right into action. When you find something lingering for a long time on your to-do list, it's a good sign that you need to do just 15 minutes to break through that block or better define the project with words that will get you started more easily.

Laps like this work well in combination with a reward. Maybe you get home and want to take the rest of the night off. Before you do, devote those few minutes to a happier home. Try setting your sights on the kitchen. Ready? Find 10 things that you don't want in your kitchen anymore. You get more bonus points the bigger they are. Kick them out to the trash, the charity box, or wherever they belong. Gone. Done. Better. That was pretty quick, wasn't it?

Trust in a quick burst when time, energy, or enthusiasm is in short supply. You put off certain chores because they seem too big to do in a small bite of your day. It's easy to view "clean the kitchen," for example, as a monumental roadblock. You don't have to do everything in a single go and even one lap can make a big difference.

Next time you're feeling daunted, say, "Okay, short burst" and make a little progress. You'll be amazed at your ability to carve a few bursts out of your day, even when you thought you didn't have a spare hour for making things nicer. Go ahead and laugh if your stubborn "don't wanna" mood evaporates and you find yourself working cheerfully long after that timer goes off. Getting started is truly the toughest bit.

Define the finish line

Be flexible in defining your laps to suit your current needs, available time, and energy. When a project needs a significant burst of effort, first take a moment to define that burst. Maybe it's "90 minutes" or "head down and work hard until my ride gets out of his meeting and is ready to go." If the project has pleasingly achievable chunks, useful progress points would be "found last year's presentation and looked through it to identify any slides to use as a base for this year's" or "read three of the five assigned articles."

Always identify a success point for a lap when working on projects that are unlikely to be fully completed during a single lap. For longer laps or daily goals, consider multiple victory conditions, such as, "finished cleaning the garage or did three laps on it *and* answered that letter from Aunt Betty." Discardian mom Erin Hare suggests a special measurement unit for parents of small children: "what can be done during one episode of *Sesame Street*."

Here's a truly magical lap. Five minutes isn't very much time out of your day, even out of the last hour before bed. You can knock something off the needs-doing list without even noticing the impact, and it's almost as if someone else flew in and made it happen. Don't plan it. Don't think about it hard. Just suddenly turn into the five-minute fairy every now and then and whisk away some annoyance from tomorrow.

3

It's All Too Much

One Bag at a Time

> There are a lot of problems here. Pick a problem
> you think you can solve, and solve it.
> —*Dr. Dave Warner, humanitarian and neuroscientist*

Just one bag

If you're feeling overwhelmed by the amount of stuff you want to clear out of your home, sometimes you'll find that it's better to do your laps by volume rather than duration. Instead of setting a timer, grab a paper grocery bag or comparably sized box and go after one category until you fill it.

Crafty crud. Many people engage in some kind of projects that involve supplies. Knitting, carpentry, building Linux servers, whatever. When one has a hobby, somehow, through a magical process, the supplies for that hobby proliferate beyond reasonable bounds. Perhaps they breed in the closets; in any case, one day (today, for instance) you realize that you have far more supplies than you've ever used since taking up the hobby. Fill up a bag with your excess craft crud. Depending on the hobby and the stuff, give it to a school or charity or throw it in a dumpster, which may be where you rescued it from in the first place.

Paper purge. Grab a paper sack and see how fast you can fill it up with recycling. Old newspapers, magazines, junk mail that didn't get properly processed when you carried it in, out-of-date coupons—the obvious stuff that you can knock out. You can also quickly fill your bag and effect some real change in your file drawers by purging user manuals for devices you no longer own, utility bills from over a year ago, and similar dead documents. (Don't forget to shred papers containing personal information.)

Evil shoes. Get a paper sack and put in all the pairs of shoes you haven't worn in the last year or that you did wear but made your feet hurt like hell every time. Maybe sell them if they're current, fashionable and in great shape or donate them. Whatever you do, get them out!

Blah books. You'll want to double-bag this paper sack; it'll be heavy. Here are some suggestions for books of which you can let go:

- Out-of-date reference, technical and travel guidebooks (if no computer in your house is running that version of that software, you do not need a book about it);

- Books you haven't opened in five years and that you don't feel like reading within the next month;

- Books you bought and intended to read, but still haven't read several years later and don't want to start this month;

- Books you didn't like;

- Books someone gave you that you don't want to read;

- Books for a hobby you no longer have; and

- Cookbooks for foods you don't eat anymore.

Check for inscriptions or papers tucked into the items you're parting with. Remember that you can keep a digital photo of a meaningful inscription, or a page on which you are quoted, and not the book itself. Putting the books in the bag does not remove them from the universe. If you later decide that you want to read one of them, odds are very good that the local library or used bookstore will have a copy—maybe even this copy—or you'll be able to get it online. A lot of books, especially nonfiction, are like oranges. Juice 'em to extract the goodness and discard the remains.

Now, what do you do with this bag once you've filled it up? Take it to a used bookstore, which buys or trades books and possibly turn it into cash or books you actually want, or you can drop it off (or at least the books that didn't sell or trade) as a donation to the library or charity.

Big warm things. A big plastic garbage bag might be better than a paper grocery bag. Go through any extra blankets and sheets, and put the ones you haven't used in the last year into the bag. Check the winter coats, scarves, gloves, sweaters, and rain boots, add any you haven't used in the last year, and take the bag down to the homeless shelter.

Toys and sporting gear. You know the drill: Get a big paper grocery sack. Today, it's toy patrol. Grownups of all sorts: You have toys, so don't think this doesn't apply to you. To those of you with kids: This can often work better if the kids help with the game of sending old toys on to a new home, and will spare their later resentment over something precious having been thrown away. Discardian and Ann Arbor community organizer Edward Vielmetti said, "My kindergartener and I did this with his bookshelves, and he picked out a bunch of books that we should save for his baby brother when he's a toddler."

With those set aside, you can donate the others. Go through the house and find the toys and sports equipment you never play with anymore. Got any little desk widgets that you're completely bored with? (Can you hear the sound of a hundred little plastic gewgaws flying into the bag around the world? Lovely, isn't it?) Did you upgrade a console game system but keep the old one, thinking that you'd break it out now and then? If it's covered in dust, send it off to a new home. How about those electronic gadgets? Anyone with more than one universal remote control, I am looking at you! Two-pound digital camera from 1999 in the back of a drawer? Ahem—bag it.

A small percentage of this stuff might worth selling on eBay or offering on craigslist, but weigh the hassle of selling against the possible outcome. It's often a better return on your time to give it away. Think of the happiness your cast-offs can bring!

Foldy clothes. Grab one of those trusty paper sacks and a trash can and head for your dressers. Purge all the clothes you don't wear anymore because they don't quite fit, are worn out, are the wrong color, etc. Trash the rags and donate the rest. This is a great exercise for the day when you desperately need to do laundry. What have you still not chosen to wear even when your choices are limited? You may find that you have a whole category of clothes heavily slanted toward the bag, so buy new ones that don't suck. You deserve nonholey socks, nonstretched-out and nonstained undershirts, and underwear that have functional elastic.

Not quite ready to wear. Revitalize your currently unusable investments! Fill a bag with clothes you like a lot and fit you, but which need to be dry cleaned, repaired, or altered. Take them to a professional and get them back into your active wardrobe. Bonus round: Take along a bag of excess wire hangers to be reused.

Pantry purge. Go through all your cupboards. Pull out anything old and nasty and put it in the trash—duh—as well as anything unopened that you aren't going to eat in the next 30 days, which should go in a bag and be taken this week to your local food bank. If you have time, pull everything out, wipe down the cupboard and dust out the cobwebs, and put back the keepers. Update the shopping list with those staples you would eat in the next 30 days if only you had enough of them.

Tupperware party. Put into a bag every plastic container you can't remember using in the last six months as well as any unmatched tops and bottoms. Charity!

Open the stasis chamber. Find a closet shelf, cupboard, or drawer that has remained largely unchanged for the last year. Fill a bag with some of that untouched stuff you don't need. Boxes that moved in with you years ago, but which you've never opened, are ideal targets for this activity. Bonus round: Use that newly cleared space as a new and better home for something that matters more to you.

One grocery bag isn't all that hard to fill, even in a tidy home, but it's actually a significant amount of space. Playing a quick round of *One Bag at a Time* is a great way to demonstrate to yourself that you have accomplished something good and you're making your world better.

Oh, No! I'm Not Perfect

The Success of a Balanced Approach

4

> Work only starts when the fear of doing nothing
> finally exceeds the fear of doing something badly.
> —*Alain de Botton, writer and entrepreneur*

Habits, projects, and dreams or desires aren't the same thing

When deciding how to invest your time and energy at work or at home, it is important to distinguish between building a habit, doing a project, and having a dream or desire. These three kinds of activities have different rules. Understand the differences and set expectations of yourself appropriately.

- *Building a habit* is a gradual process to which you commit effort and measure progress. It does not have a deadline or an end point. Making that effort and improving over time defines success.

- *Doing a project* is taking a set of steps to achieve a result. It does not necessarily have a deadline. Being currently successful with a project depends upon whether it is active or inactive. In either case, identifying the end conditions that you seek and the first action that you need to take are keys to succeeding with the project. Further, if it's an active project to which you have a current commitment, reaching those end conditions completes the definition of success.

- *Having a dream or desire* is envisioning the way your world *could* be. It does not necessarily have any associated projects or habits that might make it more likely to exist. It definitely does not have a deadline or a specific end point. Knowing whether you still want this dream or desire defines success.

Here are some examples:

- *Habit*: Putting in solid writing time every day. The only way to fail at "putting in solid writing time every day" is not to put in any solid writing time or continually put in less.

- *Project*: Writing a book. The only way to fail at "writing a book" is if it's a currently active project, not to do the next step in the project, or, if it's an inactive project, not to define it enough to know what succeeding at it would look like or what the first action for it would be.

- *Dream*: Being a writer. The only way to fail at having the dream of "being a writer" is to take action toward that dream when it's no longer what you want.

All three activities should change over time to reflect new insights, conditions, or priorities. Doing a project expects completion; building a habit *demands* action. Far too often, we unfairly treat ourselves as if every activity we undertake should lead to perfect and immediate results.

Here are some other examples:

- *Habit*: When I realize I no longer like or need something, immediately putting it in the charity box

- *Project*: Deciding the fate of the front hall stuff (then, "evaluating shoes in rack by front door" might be the next action)

- *Dream*: Having plenty of closet space

Four real choices

Deciding that you no longer want to build a particular habit, do a particular project, or have a particular dream or desire is not the same as failing. You can't do it all, so you're always making choices about where to put your energy, and that is fine.

Psychotherapist Robert L. Goulding. M.D.. taught the principle that there are four choices in any decision:

1. Do it and enjoy.

2. Do it and don't enjoy.

3. Don't do it and enjoy.

4. Don't do it and don't enjoy.

In describing this principle to me, counselor and writer (and my mother) Jinx McCombs, who studied with Dr. Goulding, said, "All four are real choices, and it's surprising how often people pick number two or number four."

What choices aren't you enjoying now that you've made them? What were the other options that you could keep in mind for next time?

Beware of cognitive bias and wrong-sized conclusions

As you evaluate your current situation, your dreams, and what you may need to discard or add, watch out for two important things: cognitive bias and over- or undersized conclusions.

Firstly, cognitive bias — a pattern of different judgment occurring for you in specific situations — can kick in when you worry about being unprepared. There is a world of difference between the overprotective response "that might come in handy for something maybe someday so I'll keep it" and specific, common-to-you situational preparation, such as "I should carry a book and writing tools when I am doing errands where I might get stuck waiting." Keep things for which you have a plan, limit the number of active plans, and limit the storage you allocate to inactive ones. Allocate your resources primarily to your current goals.

In my experience, the payoff for getting rid of 100% of the stuff for which you don't have a plan and don't wildly love is still worth it, even when you come up with a use for a small percentage of it later. Getting 90% of your unneeded items out of the way creates opportunity and energy, which makes dealing with the occasional 10% you need to get again much easier.

Beware of cognitive bias in what you notice about your things, habits, projects, and even dreams. Would it stand out in your memory that you never needed something you got rid of? No. In fact, you might forget you ever had it in the first place. That 90% can fall from your awareness without a trace, leaving the rare exceptions to stand out and seem more significant than they actually are. I highly recommend Thomas Gilovich's book, *How We Know What Isn't So: The Fallibility of Human Reason in Everyday Life*, as a great way to gain insight into some of the silly patterns of perception that can have you working against your own best interest.

Secondly, consider the scale of your conclusions about things. For example, when faced with a work environment that leaves you completely frustrated because everyone else wants to run at full speed instead of thinking in advance, it would be possible to draw the very large conclusion, "I am not suited to live in today's world."

That's a much bigger jump than the situation warrants. I'd recommend something like, "To be successful, I need to be part of a company culture that fits more in the middle or to the planned side of the over-planned versus winging-it continuum." That's a life lesson on which you can act for future job decisions. It certainly gives you a good answer to the old "Is there anything you'd like to know about us?" question in a job interview!

The opposite pattern—undersized conclusions—is also worth your attention. Folks who are overly hard on themselves will often discount their efforts in achieving a particular situation, saying, "I just got lucky." instead of "That worked out great! I should approach similar problems that way again and see if it helps." Listen to the language you use with yourself and keep it in line with what achieves positive change in your world.

Balancing your commitments

We all have pet projects, social commitments, goals for personal or professional growth, and hobbies to which we devote our time. We stroll past the buffet of life and load our plates. Unfortunately, we make a lot of trips back to that smorgasbord of options and, pretty soon, we are groaning under the load.

Do you really like everything you picked up thinking it would be tasty? Can you really finish all that? Would doing so leave you feeling painfully overstuffed?

Look at your obligations, including those things on which you aren't spending time but which weigh on your mind as well as where the hours of your day go. Think about how you would prioritize that list. What can you get rid of because you don't want it anymore? What should you abandon because it isn't as desirable as the other things on your plate?

Waving bye-bye

When you decide to drop or deactivate a project, take time to close it. If you have physical materials that you won't want or need anymore, decide their fate and send them away. Take a picture of that unfinished painting (or whatever) to document how far you got, and maybe write some notes about why you chose that project and why you're now parting with it.

If it's something less tangible—say, participation in a club for which you don't have time anymore—write a thank-you and farewell letter or make a call to conclude your involvement. Acknowledge the good in the activity and then move to a higher priority. If it was something you added to your plate just for yourself, such as, "I will learn Swahili in my spare time" or "I will read an entire new book every week"—make some kind of parting gesture to confirm that this item isn't just fading down to the bottom of your current list but is coming off that list. It is not still floating out there as an obligation anymore.

Know what you want to be doing now

You'll be less stressed if you have a clear head and a good picture of what's on your current list. Acknowledge things on which you might want to work in the future and realize that they are *not* a current priority. For things that are active now, prioritize them; if the list is at all overwhelming, move the bottom items into an inactive status.

Begin your efforts with what's at the top of your list, whether it's a habit, a project, or a goal by creating a new active habit or project. Based on your available time and energy, put in chunks of effort toward the things on your list and work in order.

> At the top of the list, put things on which you want to work daily and restart at the top of the list every day. Some days you will make it farther down the list than other days. That's fine, as long as you keep the list arranged according to your priorities.
>
> Good progress isn't perfect completion of everything; it is steady, prioritized time and effort toward what matters to you most.

If you beat yourself up over what's not done, remember that all your possible projects need to happen in their season and when your energy, time, and priorities permit. It's like gardening; accept that it can't all get done at once. Can't rake the autumn leaves in the spring, right?

Build in time to take care of you

When you're setting priorities, consider goals or desires you may have such as "be less stressed," "have more fun," or "feel healthier." Remember that progress comes from creating habits and projects to support them. It is vital to acknowledge consciously that these enjoyable things are also your priorities, and you can devote time and effort to them without feeling like you're failing in other areas. You do not need to account for everything that happens in the universe. The rest of the world will get on fine without you while you take that half hour to build a couch cushion fort with your nieces, meditate, or walk in the park.

———

Sudden stuff will come up. When this happens, if it really isn't a higher priority than the other things in your queue, prioritize it and do it at the appropriate time, giving whoever is bringing it to you a realistic prediction of when you'll get to it (and, if needed, an understanding of the stuff that has to be cleared from your plate beforehand). Chug on through.

Maybe you won't get very far down the list, but you'll know what's going on and work on the right things first instead of the noisiest or immediate fun.

When working on any activity, be fair with yourself over what you can achieve with that chunk of time and energy. Start and be focused. Don't stress about not completing everything in one 30-minute lap. Make progress, enjoy it, and move to the next priority. Over time, you'll become better at estimating how much time and energy things take and setting expectations, with both yourself and others.

As you learn how long things take, you'll grow more confident about letting them stray from optimal conditions. As David Allen put it, "Freedom to create a mess is proportional to your ability to know what 'no mess' is and how to get there."

As you practice Discardia, you'll get a sense of how long it will take to make a room feel comfortable and unchaotic once again. This is a great talent because it will reduce your stress over minor clutter and help you stay focused on implementing deeper changes. Parents will find this skill useful in telling the difference between spending half an hour tidying after they tuck in the kids and making bigger changes.

You can bring your Discardian habits to a comfortable point that you trust. Then, you can rest within a tidal pattern where your routines of decluttering and mindful relaxation wash away debris and return you to a calm, peaceful smoothness.

5

Uh-oh. Did I Remember to Worry About Forgetting That?

Offboard Memory

> There are three things I always forget. Names,
> faces, and—the third I can't remember.
> —*Italo Svevo, novelist*

Don't be so worried about forgetting things

As you get older, there will be moments when you can't remember something, but that's hardly surprising when you think about it. The older you get, the more information and experiences you've taken in. It doesn't seem odd to me that it would grow more difficult to pull a particular fact out of an ever-increasing pile of other facts.

Today, take some time to think about that which you do remember now and want to keep remembering later. We humans have an amazing memory tool for this: *writing*. There's that speech trick, too, which is also handy.

- Label and name the people in your old photos.

- Take pictures of beloved possessions with a story behind them and write the story to keep with the image. Blogs and photo-sharing sites like Flickr are particularly handy for this.

- Talk into a tape recorder or an audioblog service like Hipcast and tell the stories you remember, even if they're not associated with a physical souvenir.

- Tell your stories in person to family and friends.

Most of all, don't give yourself a hard time about not remembering every single thing you've ever done, heard, read or otherwise encountered. It'd be a pretty poor and dull life if the human brain could every detail. Put the things that really matter to you in some form of offboard backup and relax.

Set up memory safety nets

Have someone else remember something for you. Enjoy the beauty of those three magic words: "automatic minimum payment." Talk with the companies behind all your monthly bills and see if there's a way to have the minimum payment automatically charged to your bank account or credit card.

The key word here is "minimum." You should pay more if you can to avoid interest charges, but always pay the least possible amount to avoid late fees. Then, while you have them on the phone, see if you can get your bills by email. This keeps paper from landing in your house and gives you the earliest possible warning if a bill amount is in error.

Plan ahead and make checklists or kits to ensure repeatedly that you have what you need when and where you need it. When you travel, for example, think ahead and bring the stuff you wind up kicking yourself for forgetting.

- Bring your own comfortable headphones and, ideally, a music player with your own tunes to give you aural privacy.

- Acknowledge in advance that airlines may not provide anything worth eating and that the airport food choices will be fair to middling at high prices. Pack a lunch or at least bring some good snacks from home.

- Tuck one or two of those magazines you've been meaning to read into your bag or print out a long article from the web. You'll get something off the stack at home and won't have to suffer through an "It'll do" choice from the airport newsstand. (If the magazines have overpoweringly scented perfume inserts, tear those out before you travel and tuck them in the bottom of your kitchen trash or in the compost. Travel is headache inducing enough!)

- Staying in a hotel for business? Don't drink the tiny $5 water bottle in the room. Instead, take a walk over to the nearest grocery or drug store and buy a big bottle for half that price. Your legs could use the stretch and you'll see a little of the outside world in a new place.

- Leave one dose of painkillers or other frequently used medications in your bag. Why suffer the hassle of hunting for some when you already have a headache?

These travel principles can apply to your life back home, too. Always need a pen in the car and don't ever have one? Round up a dozen pens and put them in the glove compartment along with a film canister or other little container for meter change. Often caught sniffling without a tissue? Carry a handkerchief, and throw some hand sanitizer in your bag to help avoid some of those colds. Constantly scrambling for the transit fare? Keep that fare amount and $20 —enough for an emergency taxi ride—separate from the rest of your cash in your wallet. Set yourself up for smooth sailing even when the seas get rough.

———

Don't give yourself a hard time for not keeping things in your head. Make a list. Your brain isn't meant to carry all that stuff around; it's meant for thinking and working on the stuff on your list. Keep some index cards or other small note-taking supplies with you and put them next to the phone and the computer. Write yourself notes. Leave yourself voicemails. Send yourself emails. It's fine.

No one remembers everything. Really.

Procrastination

Bottom Line: Deeds are Better

6

> Joining a Facebook group about creative
> productivity is like buying a chair about jogging.
> —*Merlin Mann, productivity guru and humorist*

You have a choice

Ah, procrastination: the villain in so many stories of the great adventures we might have had—if only. Here's what's certain: You do not always in the moment want to do what you know most serves your goals in the big picture. You drag your feet, check email and social messaging services "just once more," follow that link to the funny YouTube video, flip through magazines or TV channels, anything but buckle down to the task in front of you.

Procrastination is an act of denial. It is pretending that you don't care to achieve something. The key to conquering procrastination is to perceive it, see it for what it is, and recognize that you are making a conscious choice.

Once you know that you're a making a choice, you can, at minimum, increase the satisfaction provided by whatever it is you *do* instead of what you *should* be doing. Instead of aimlessly filling time avoiding a task, take a conscious timeout to do something that will bring you real pleasure.

If you aren't going to accomplish the task you think is most important, at least accomplish *something* that's on your list. Around my house, we call this "procrastaproductivity," which can be a highly effective way to knock a lot of things off your to-do list when there's something daunting at the top. It's amazing how attractive chores can become when you're avoiding another task, but don't let yourself put that tough thing off for too long or you'll continually be stressed about what you are not accomplishing. For every few things you do further down your list, put in a short lap on that big scary one at the top.

Beware of spending so much time trying to come up with the perfect tool or method to do something that you never actually start. Nerds are particularly prone to this pattern of avoidance, sometimes spending hours trying to find the best software for a task that's easier to do physically than digitally, or wasting days fiddling with the configuration of their tools. Ironically, a cheap and rudimentary tool can sometimes encourage use more than a highly polished one because it sets the best balance between "good enough" and "not too good to tinker with." An example of this is setting up a shelf in your office to hold grouped papers or other items relating to active projects and labeling the edge of the shelf below each group with a sticky note. The casualness of the labeling removes any hesitancy about rearranging, eliminating, or adding groups.

Don't sweat the how more than the what. Push aside that creative futzing around and move things forward. Step away from the distractions of the web and TV, and whatever other shininess keeps you from tackling your top priority, and put in a solid chunk of effort—15 minutes, half an hour, or an hour—just run one lap.

Right now. Get up and handle the damn thing. Do it, decide not to do it, or break it down to multiple less cringe-worthy tasks. Really, it won't take *that* long. Just deal with it. *It's time.*

The man with the hammer

Whether you're in familiar or alien territory, it's often tempting to dawdle over those finishing touches trying to make sure that everything is exactly right before you release the results of your work into the world. The artist John Nordstrand said that a work of art requires both an artist and "the man with the hammer" whose job it is to hit the artist when it's time to quit tweaking and call the piece done. Watch for the time to change your role from one to the other. What are you going to declare done today and get out the door (literally or metaphorically)?

Bounce onto it

Got a task you keep putting off? Do it the moment you come back through the door without letting anything else distract you. Whether you are returning from errands, walking into your office in the morning, or coming home at the end of the day, keep that momentum rolling right over that beastly old chore.

Here are some common culprits that require lighting a fire under your butt and doing a lap to break through the procrastination barrier:

Taxes and other bureaucratic chores. Take care of one tedious bureaucratic chore that has been lingering on your list. Make that appointment to renew your driver's license, set up direct deposit for your paychecks with your payroll department at work, and refill those prescriptions—whatever will give you that lovely "Phew! That's finally done" feeling.

Start by pulling together all the papers or information you need to do the task. It usually takes less time than you think but, if you have to stop before doing the rest of the task, at least you've made it much easier to finish tomorrow. Take advantage of online services that can streamline what you need to do. I'm a big fan of TurboTax's online service, for example.

With regard to taxes, there are three possible outcomes to preparing them early: you get your refund early; or you figure out that you don't have to pay a significant amount or you have extra time to budget for a large amount owed. They are all better than waiting to know until the due date. It is astonishing to realize there can be a big payoff from some of these bureaucratic chores. When finally filling out that health care claim, which could result in a big reimbursement check, don't forget it's a pretty good hourly wage for sitting down and taking care of it!

Living healthier. Promenading along the shore of denial is not an exercise plan. You know that you want to feel and look great. You know that eating better and moving more will help you achieve this. Find the intersection between what you like and what you want to be doing.

> Do a healthy activity you enjoy—say, watching movies or surfing the web while walking on a treadmill—and eat a healthy food you like every day.

If you have to motivate yourself with something other than the benefit of feeling and looking better, write a big check (or a letter volunteering your time) to charity and give it to a trusted friend who will mail it if you haven't achieved certain workout goals you've set for yourself. If a pain in your wallet stirs you into action more than the size of the butt next to it, by all means, use what works!

Building something really great with someone. Don't hold yourself back waiting for the big, perfect gesture to deepen your friendship or show your deeper affection. Acknowledge special occasions, but remember that tiny threads stitch together relationships. Go ahead and do that small kindness for no special reason. Out-of-the-blue sweetness counts for more in most people's book than the regimentally remembered birthday card.

The worst room. At home, what room is the biggest mess? Where's the core of your physical chaos? Give it 30 minutes of focused attention today. Maybe it's such a disaster that all you can do is write down the plan of all the steps that need to happen to recover that space. That's okay; just be sure you use all 30 minutes and get started on Step #1 as soon as you can. My friend, entrepreneur Mena Trott, was inspired when her husband was off on a trip. She surprised him on his return with a beautiful new sitting room that she'd unearthed under the stacks of boxes, junk mail, and random crud that had piled up in their spare room. A whole extra room in your home for the price of some cleaning up and maybe a couple of pieces of new (or new to you) furniture to round out the new look? That's a deal!

Getting fancy. Is there something about which you keep thinking, "Gee, someday it'd be fun to get all dressed up and go to that place?" Stop putting it off! Make time to make that daydream come true. Why delay any longer something that could be a savored memory for years? Catch that exhibit at the museum before it leaves town. See that movie with a friend. Eat at the great restaurant that you've wanted to try. Take that big walk through the park.

Optimize your daily suckage. Find the worst daily hassle and give it a nudge toward less awful. Maybe you need to replace or repair an essential tool, improve your surroundings for a tedious task, or begin a project to upgrade the whole situation that necessitates this activity. Whatever will make future occasions better, brainstorm to find options for yourself, improve where you can, and, whenever possible, dump the worst, soul-sapping suckage.

That long-delayed to-do. What's gotta get handled around your world? Maybe it's a chore, maybe it's a play you want to see before it closes, maybe it's a phone call you've been putting off, or maybe it's getting the hell out of the house and taking some time for yourself so you don't go stark-raving mad. Pause and see what pressure on you needs to be relieved, and then take care of it. Closure creates energy and un-closed loops steal energy. What can you finish next? On what would you really like to move ahead with that fresh burst of energy?

———

If you can't resist delaying something, procrastinate on procrastination. Say, "I'll get back to putting this off in just a moment, but first a quick lap."

7

I Don't Wanna!

A Spoonful of Sugar

> Do whatever it takes to make your life more worth
> living. Anything at all. Just don't be mean.
> —*Kate Bornstein, writer and performance artist*

Lure yourself into positive action

Sometimes procrastination is active and you find yourself internally kicking like a three year old and throwing a tantrum at the mere notion of doing things that must be done. How do you conquer this brat? The brat is nearsighted and pessimistic, so you need to pull back to a bigger picture and see your positive options.

Instead of beating yourself up with the "you *must*" stick, lure your most stubborn self into positive action with two carrots: the relief of avoiding unpleasant hassles in the future and an upgraded way of approaching things in the present.

For example, when you walk into the kitchen and are faced with a sink full of dirty dishes from the last few days, recognize that putting off washing them will make your house smell nasty, and they'll certainly be more unpleasant to deal with later. Before you do them, though, open a window to get a nice breeze in the room, maybe put on some music you like, or pour a nice beverage to sip as the dishwater heats up.

Now, glance at the clock and then do the dishes without looking at it again. As you do the dishes, figure out what you *do* like about this task, such as splashing in the water, feeling the warmth, or having the satisfaction of transforming filthy and foul to fine and clean. The best sinks have a window to see what the outside world has to report as you go about your work (and the lack of that at the apartment we rent now has made me note it as a desired feature of our next place, if we ever move!).

When you're done, look at the clock again. It doesn't take that long—many less than 20 minutes—to do most chores. You can blow 20 minutes without even thinking about it by watching TV or surfing the web. A lot of things that you have to do don't really take that much out of your day and needn't be put off.

Make it a game

If you can find a way to make it more of a game, many things become more fun and you'll be more inclined to work on them. That's the principle behind EpicWin, an iPhone app that you can use to cajole yourself into doing mundane household chores: "I really want to call it quits for the night, but washing the dishes will only take five minutes and I'll get experience points for it. I'm really close to leveling up!" HealthMonth, the online game, helps build habits that will make you feel better all the time. It's not just a silly trick. Games designer, researcher, and author Jane McGonigal cites years of scientific studies to back up her assertion that "... when we game we are tapping into our best qualities: our ability to be motivated, to be optimistic, to collaborate with others, to be resilient in the face of failure."

Stepping into that place of strength in the safe environment of games makes it easier for us to do so outside of them. Bringing elements of games, which amplify those positive aspects of ourselves into the rest of our lives, can help us win in the real world.

McGonigal used game principles to help her recover from a concussion, figuring that when you're sick you aren't yourself so why not be someone awesome? She imagined herself as Jane the Concussion Slayer and invited friends to take the functions of Buffy's allies in the show that inspired her. Together they found and fought the bad guys (the triggers for her symptoms), identified her "power-ups" (those things she could still do that made her feel good), and worked on her superhero to-do list (not merely trying to get back to normal—*boring!*—but getting to extraordinary). Did it work? Yes! She saw improvements within the first 30 days and was almost fully recovered a year later. Best of all, she stopped suffering because she had something actionable to do about her situation. Now she shares the technique in her game called SuperBetter, which is helping people all around the world remember that even though pain may be inevitable, suffering is optional.

Be creative and playful as you find ways to fight nonawesome crap in your life! You don't have to get complicated to feel these benefits. Take advantage of even your worst qualities by playing sneaky tricks on yourself. For example, I sat down to a 40-minute podcast that I'd been planning to hear, and set some mending in my lap as it began. Easily distracted, I barely noticed what my hands were doing and was finished with that long-procrastinated chore well before the podcast was over!

Stay pleased

Think about what you choose instead when you don't want to do what you know you should do. Notice that some of these things may be optional, taking a lot of your time and yet providing minimal reward or enjoyment. At this point, I turn and look pointedly at the TV and the computer. Don't fill your time with unrewards *and* procrastination. Find the things that please you and do them instead of things that provide you with nothing.

Fans of C.S. Lewis's *The Screwtape Letters* are here encouraged to go reread Letter Thirteen, which includes this bit of admonition from a senior devil to a junior tempter:

> But you were trying to damn your patient by the World, that is by palming off vanity, bustle, irony, and expensive tedium as pleasures. How can you have failed to see that a real pleasure was the last thing you ought to have let him meet? Didn't you foresee that it would just kill by contrast all the trumpery which you have been so laboriously teaching him to value? And that the sort of pleasure which the book and the walk gave him was the most dangerous of all? That it would peel off from his sensibility the kind of crust you have been forming on it, and make him feel that he was coming home, recovering himself?

Do what you love whenever you can. Even if the busyness of life only gives you a few minutes—my sympathies to you new parents out there—make good use of it and don't put off activities that matter to you. Read a chapter of a book, practice that guitar, cuddle with your sweetheart, plant a few bulbs in the garden, or look through the bulb catalog and think about what you'd like to get—whatever feeds your soul. When you have to do something that you wouldn't otherwise choose to do for pleasure or growth, find the parts of the experience that give you some kind of payoff and supplement it if you can with something you *would* choose, like music you really enjoy. You are going to be where you are now and you are not always going to be doing things that are fun, so make the best that you can of all your moments.

8 The Giant Plan for the Rest of My Life

Agile Self Development

> Contrary to what some "gurus" will tell you, there is no single, life-changing secret to working less and living more. The reality is that small changes practiced over time yield big results.
> — *Gina Trapani, writer and developer*

Iterate and improve

One of my key beliefs is that personal growth happens most effectively as a series of small, incremental changes. When there is a huge, daunting goal, our little monkey brains often freak out and nothing gets done. The mountain just seems too high to climb. As a personal coach, I've learned that I can effectively help people make these changes by using some of the same techniques used in agile software development. These techniques help teams make a little bit of software at a time and then combine those bits, building it into something more full featured while making adjustments and changes along the way.

What is "agile software development"?

Agile, a lightweight methodology used for writing software, emerged under that name around a decade ago. It is a natural set of tools to adapt to personal growth. It originated as a reaction against older approaches that rely on a very large amount of detailed, inflexible preplanning and supporting documentation of those plans.

Software developer Christian Nelson describes the agile approach as "iterative, adaptive, collaborative, and reality-based." Agile software development creates usable results more quickly than older methods and then continuously improves those results while keeping them functional. This approach allows the team to adapt readily to changing information and requirements by regularly measuring progress against estimates and reflecting on effectiveness, tuning and adjusting accordingly.

So what is "agile *self* development"?

Agile self development is a lightweight methodology used for personal development and a reaction against all-or-nothing goals, resolutions, and productivity systems. I began developing it in 2010 and presented it at South By Southwest (SXSW) Interactive technology conference in 2011 with fellow coach Marcy Swenson. It enables geeks to repurpose tools they already know, and we're hopeful that the community practicing it will evolve from its current beginnings.

What does agile self development do? Same as agile in the software world (that is, creates early and continuous valuable results; adapts readily to changing information and requirements; regularly measures progress against estimates; and reflects on effectiveness, tuning, and adjusting accordingly). Best of all, thanks to the iterative and self-examining nature of this approach, constantly improving your happiness and personal fulfillment reveals ever better ways to do so. It creates an upward spiral of positive change.

Agile self development celebrates:

- Increasing individual productivity and satisfaction using whatever method works more than adhering to a specific system;

- Quality of life more than quantity of achievement;

- Small, quick decision making that works toward current goals more than detailed, long-term planning;

- Simplicity more than complexity; and

- Responding to change more than following a script.

How to do agile self development sprints

A sprint is a not-too-big chunk of time during which you'll focus on a limited list of priorities. In practice, a series of sprints allow you to correct and adjust as you learn from each one.

You can approach a sprint with these simple steps:

1. **What is your big, exciting vision?** What is it that you want to create, do, or be? Agile self development will help you get there, although the "there" may change along the way.

2. **What are all the ways you could start?** This is your chance to brainstorm and pour out all of the possibilities. (3x5 cards come in handy here, although making a list on paper is fine. If you're around other folks, this is a great time to ask for suggestions.)

3. **Which of these possibilities will yield immediate results, is do-able now, and uses your current skills, abilities, and will-power?** Whatever you choose will be what you're going to work on for the first sprint. You also need to choose a sprint length (a week, two weeks, or a month are common durations).

4. **What can you measure to know if you're making progress (that is, your velocity)?** Examples would be whether you actually did something, how many minutes you did it for each day, how you felt at the end of the day, how many people you talked to about something, or how many hours you slept. Find something meaningful to measure, and then make an estimate of how you think things will go. Measurement leads to mindfulness.

5. **Now, start the sprint!** Go! Have fun with the experiment and keep that "quality of life" part in mind.

One useful technique with which to experiment is the daily standup. In agile software development this is a very quick meeting—so short that you don't even need to sit down—where everyone on a team checks in with each other. The daily standup is an opportunity to ask the questions, "What did I do yesterday? What will I do today? Am I blocked?" This can happen with supportive buddies or through a brief time spent writing. The latter can combine well with the "daily pages" concept frequently mentioned in books on becoming a writer (and is thus an example of grabbing from anywhere tools and patterns that work for you and blending them into your own useful combination).

6. **At the end of the sprint, conduct a retrospective.** You can have it by yourself, write about it online or in a journal, or invite a buddy to talk about how things went. Buddies are always nice and they provide perspective, which is why some people love working in pairs. During your retrospective, ask:

- How did it go?

- How accurate was my estimate?

- What did I learn about the world and myself?

- What was the Awesome (the thing that went unexpectedly well)?

- What was the Mystery (the thing I can't yet explain)?

- What will I change for the next sprint? (This could be a small adjustment or huge pivot to a new idea.)

A sprint example

The goal of doing sprints is to update continually the experiment to move you closer to your vision, which could change over time, and to learn in the process. We'll look at this idea further in Part Four, "December Discardia: Core Principle #3—Perpetual Upgrade." One of the best things about an agile approach is that it produces both early tangible results *and* learning.

Here's an example: Imagine someone whose vision is of a light-filled, uncluttered, top-floor apartment instead of her current dark and dreary basement. She knows she doesn't currently have the savings to move, so how can she use agile self development to make progress toward that goal over the next month?

She gets out a blank piece of paper and brainstorms many ways—practical and silly—to get her closer to her dream. Then she circles the ones she could start doing right now. From those, she picks a couple for this sprint and makes an appointment with herself in her calendar for one month in the future to hold a retrospective and review her progress.

She's going to work on her debt by reducing her spending and not using her credit card. That's easily measurable—and she can note in that calendar appointment the current numbers to save herself time when comparing later.

One of her uncircled ideas was to "get a raise," which isn't fully under her control, but she realizes that she can influence it. She decides to check the date of her next review, look back at what her boss wanted to see in the way of improvement at the last one, and then find ways to demonstrate her progress in those areas. On her work calendar, she books half an hour in each of the next four weeks to focus on that. She can measure herself against those review goals.

Her last focus area is to start eliminating junk that doesn't need to move to the new apartment. She sets up a charity box and empties the trash and recycling. Then, every time she notices something that isn't in her vision of her new place, she can immediately move it into one of those outbound bins. Measurement here is simply how much she gets rid of and how her mood improves as the current place becomes less cluttered.

Applying agile self development to Discardia

Good so far? Now how can we apply agile self development to a Discardian holiday? Let's start with imagining an excellent last day of this Discardia cycle. That's another way of saying, "I'm defining a sprint of now until [whenever the current Discardia holiday ends], and I'm brainstorming the touchstone for a successful, valuable sprint."

Imagine what your state of mind would be on that day. Envision a valuable outcome, and then examine possible choices—with that touchstone in mind, allowing you to eliminate things that won't provide the outcome you're seeking. After that, if necessary, do some rough ranking to reduce your options to a nonoverwhelming number on which you could work during this sprint. Then, pick a few goals—three is usually a good number—from the ones about which you're most excited.

Why set more than one goal within a sprint? *Agility!* Our rebellious monkey brains don't like to be told what to do all the time—monkeys don't like leashes—so support your ability to shift into your current and most effective gear. In essence, regularly ask, "What is best for me to do now with my available resources, context, and energy?" (If that sounds like David Allen's "Getting Things Done" (GTD) approach, well, there's the "use the tools and tricks from anywhere that work best for you" principle in action again!) Even if you're stalled on one front, you can shift gears and make progress on another.

By not making an enormous plan that attempts to account for every possibility in the world, which will of course be blindsided by unexpected events, and instead working in more focused, shorter sprints, you can be relaxed and ready to respond to whatever emerges that matches your vision for yourself.

One attendee at our session at SXSW said, "I've stopped trying to smash doors through brick walls, and instead I now look for the open doors before me."

Be nice to your future self—in the sense of taking information you have at hand now and putting it where you'll need it later, and setting measurable, achievable points of progress in the direction you want to move. Compassion, kindness, self-awareness, and reflection are blessings you can give yourself with this approach.

Marketing and social media director Sabrina Caluori summed it up well: "So freaking simple. Envision the outcome you want. But leave options. Be agile. Allow yourself to adjust in the moment."

9

Worrying About Your Bottom

Start at the Top Again

> We can give ourselves nights and weekends if we
> stop confusing tasking with working.
> —*T.R. Warren, business consultant*

The 80/20 rule

In your work life or when buckling down to personal projects, it's easy to keep the truly important things from getting done by spending too much time at the bottom of your to-do list. Setting overall priorities is the foundation to making good choices about what to do. You need to know what matters a lot to you to realize when you're wasting time on things that don't.

As a general principle, spend 80% of your time on the 20% most important activities. The corollary to this is that 80% of what will fall onto your plate is not a priority. That doesn't necessarily mean that you can discard it all, but some of it can be scratched off your list and the rest can be postponed until the important stuff is done. What matters most is to be doing something in that top 20% more of the time than not.

Acknowledge the allure of completion and resist doing so much quick busywork that you fail to move your most important projects forward. The hope for an easy win can keep us coming back to our email inboxes to see what has arrived in the past few minutes. Before we spend any chunk of time questing for inbox zero, we need to look for and do the next actions from our goals.

Picking three "Most Important Things"

Discardia is a framework. One of the things I've frequently bolted onto mine is blogger and author Leo Babauta's idea of picking three "Most Important Things" for each day. Ideally, these should be derived from the top goals for your top priorities.

> Pick your three things before looking at email. Then scan quickly for anything that might need to be traded for one of the three you picked, and get to work right away on what matters. This is also a great Friday afternoon exercise. Leave yourself a note on your desk with the three things you want to accomplish Monday and then start switching into your off-duty thinking by identifying three things that you'd like to have happen over the weekend.

Getting stuff out of your head and safely parked somewhere in your system—whether paper or digital—combined with picking today's few priorities is vastly more productive than perfect fiddly management of all possible tasks.

Shiny buckets

As I maintain my list of goals and priorities, one visual image to which I keep returning is a set of shiny silver buckets and big heavy rubber balls to put in them. The buckets represent my priorities, my core values, and the roles I play; all of which defines who I really am and want to be. The balls are the goals I have right now in relation to those priorities. I can't hold very many buckets at once—certainly seven would be the maximum and that would require three hooked on each arm and one handle gripped in my teeth! The more balls I put in each bucket the fewer buckets I can hold.

The ridiculousness of the image of that physical burden helps remind me not to overload myself mentally. I can choose a manageable amount of stuff to be actively working on now, knowing that I will add new balls or swap out the buckets as I finish with these.

Having trouble identifying those buckets? Think about who you want to be, and about the roles you want to play for yourself and in the lives of those around you. Choose three things you want and three things you don't want in your life. Think big. Don't edit what your heart and gut are telling you; it's the truth of your wanting, which will fuel your change in the right direction. Something that sounds little and achievable, of which you basically like the idea, will not lead to as much positive growth as burning for something huge that you're afraid you can never have.

You can change your choices later, but choose something now. *Pick a road and get moving.*

Next time you have an option—and we are faced with options all day long—make sure that, whenever possible, you're going for things that fit the want list and avoiding things leading to the don't-want list.

Juggling

The details of which top thing to do are insignificant compared to the impact of staying focused on the key stuff. As you meet goals and your situation shifts, the items in that top 20% will change. Things that are currently lower down may move up, and things in the top may move down. Don't stress about these undulations or spend more time maintaining your to-do list than doing what's on it. It's like juggling: Intentionally dropping one of the balls to the ground while kicking a new one up into the pattern isn't failure—it's flexibility.

What's most important is to stay in tune with what is at the top of the list and keep returning to that instead of to items lower down. The best times to work on lower priority tasks are when you've cleared the higher priorities out of the way (or are waiting for other people in order to be able to proceed) or when time, energy level, or resources are inadequate for your higher priority tasks.

In my to-do tracker (using the OmniFocus software), I have a context called *braindead*, as well as more traditional ones like phone *calls* or *errands*, which I use to identify things I can still accomplish when I'm feeling pretty useless. It happens to the best of us. As David Allen said, "When in doubt (or when on one of those politically mandated conference calls), clean a drawer."

It's absolutely fine to consider temporal convenience as you prioritize. Respect the undulations in your energy. Sometimes you need to recharge. Let your pendulum swing where it needs to be and always watch for ways you can better support yourself at your less competent times of the day.

The one-week priority exercise

Here's an exercise you can do regularly to realign yourself to the top of your list. It is geared toward those with a manager and some degree of autonomy; however, even if you're self-employed or fairly constrained in how you spend your workday, you can use it as a model for consciously steering a small amount of your daily time toward improving your situation. Each day for a week, you'll be focusing on two priorities.

Day 1

Work (or, for the retired and students, projects you do for others). Carve 20 minutes out of your day somewhere (or stay late, or come in early tomorrow if you have to) to think hard about a few things. Take a few notes to identify:

- The projects your boss most wants you to have completed (and which, therefore, can have an impact on your chance of a raise);

- The project which nags at you most and which it will relieve you greatly to have completed;

- The projects your boss has been waiting for you to complete that can be finished in less than an hour;

- The projects that will most help you be more efficient in the future; and

- A demonstration of the required skills for the position to which you'd like to be promoted.

You're going to come back to these each day for the rest of the week, so keep these high-level categories in mind as you work through the days.

Home. Find that uncompleted project that is taking up the most space. Spend 45 minutes on it, pack it up for storage with a note to remind yourself of the next steps to do, or officially abandon it and get it out of the way.

Day 2

Work. Today go back to "the projects your boss wants you to have completed." First, figure out the status and the next step. Second, if you can complete the next step in less than 30 minutes, do so; otherwise, identify what needs to happen before you can move it forward. Third, email a status report to your boss, such as, "Hi, I thought you'd be interested in an update on what's happening with this project ..." Make sure it covers current status, next step, any actions required by others to move it forward, and when you expect to be able to do that step or meet with others to get it rolling. Be concise; bosses really like having a clear picture from a very brief message.

Home. Find all the open projects that are taking up more than a shoebox or a binder's space. Jot them down on paper. Mull them over a little. Circle the ones that still matter to you. Put a star by the ones on which you'd enjoy working tomorrow if you suddenly and magically had a completely free day. Draw a dotted line through the ones that don't matter to you anymore.

Day 3

Work. Yes, yes, indeed! The time has come to slap down "the project which nags at you most and which it will relieve you greatly to have completed." Don't let it take over your day if it would cause other issues, but do put in at least 30 minutes and move that horrid old festering project closer to being out of your life.

Home. Clean up, get rid of, or pass along one of the projects through which you drew a dotted line on yesterday's list. Cross it off now. Reward yourself with a little chunk of time working on one of your starred projects. Even if you only have time to look at it and write down a little list of what you want to do next, that's great. It is nice to think about a fun project as you head off to bed.

Day 4

Work. It's time to put in some progress on "the projects your boss has been waiting for you to complete that can be finished in less than an hour." See if you can knock out two of these—even one is good—without negatively impacting other important things. Be sure to send an email to your boss reporting any significant progress.

Home. Clean up and optimize your project space for a bit this evening. Good progress would include vacuuming or sweeping if that area has become less pleasant. Does it need to change to make it easier for you to work on things in comfort? What would make the space more inviting to sit down in and move things forward at last?

Day 5

Work. Carve out at least 30 minutes today to work on something that results in "a demonstration of the required skills for the position to which you'd like to be promoted." Good candidates are things like giving better presentations, being able to succinctly and effectively summarize a lot of information, writing clearly (particularly valuable for technical folks but also great for anyone who has to articulate what their organization is doing or hoping to do), and being a mentor.

Home. Get rid of or pass along another of those projects through which you put a dotted line on your list, and cross it off for good. I recommend the one that is taking up the most space or the space you most want to be using for other things. Again, look at the starred projects and think about what you might want to work on this weekend. Is there a project you'd love to work on that's waiting for some supplies or other errand to move it forward? Weekends have opportunities for such things. Mmm, weekends ...

Days 6 and 7

Work. What? Work on a weekend? Yes, because this time I want you to do something that doesn't necessarily relate to your present job but to your ability to do jobs in general well and with less stress. Stroll on down to the library or your local bookstore and get your hands on one of these books or something else that's been recommended to help build the skills you want:

- *Getting Things Done* by David Allen (to help prioritize your time)

- *Don't Sweat The Small Stuff* or *Don't Sweat The Small Stuff At Work* by Richard Carlson (to help with general stress reduction)

- *Wishcraft* by Barbara Sher (to help identify what you really want to be doing)

Home. Yay! You have time to work on a project if you want, I hope. Or you could go to the movies or take a long bath. Whatever ... enjoy!

Focus

Pay attention to real, top priorities. Clear your mental clutter. When you're doing something, you're choosing not to be doing other things. That's fine. You can do anything—just not everything. You want to choose what to do in line with your overall vision for yourself. Pick three active goals for your projects to serve. Choose just one habit to form. However you set your priorities—whether by targeting specific important qualities like, "What will best demonstrate my performance to my boss?" or, "What will help me feel most happy and relaxed this weekend?" or by putting all your goals and projects in order—keep your time and effort flowing mostly to the top of the list. You'll find yourself more energized and more successful in achieving even your biggest goals.

———

What does it take to do something big? Just one chunk at a time, but you have to start. *Now.*

Part Two

June Discardia: Core Principle #1— Decide and Do

Get a little perspective

You can use Discardia in June as a trampoline to give you a big bounce forward and break up patterns of stagnation. This holiday period is about solving entropy by making choices and acting on them. You've gotten your solid ground in place and given yourself a good footing. Now it's time to jump, knowing that your landing is already prepared.

- What's dragging you down or holding you back?

- Where is your energy going?

- Is your energy fueling your engines or just polluting your world?

Take a good hard look at the patterns in your life right now, decide what you want to change, and begin those changes. As Discardian and fine-art painter Laurel McBrine said, "Refusing to do some things sets you free to do what you really want or need to do."

	SYMPTOM
10	**Hello, Same Old Bad Habit**
	SOLUTION
	Transform It!

It is easier to act yourself into a new way of thinking
than to think yourself into a new way of acting.
—*E. Stanley Jones, missionary and theologian*

Finding ways to change

Habits are not something we change overnight. Successfully replacing a bad habit (one that interferes with you being the person you want to be) with a good habit (one that helps you progress toward your goals) requires cutting yourself a little slack.

It's not going to happen immediately or bring 100% success. At the same time as we are being patient and understanding with ourselves, we have to be relentless. Habits change through daily effort and consistent pressure to take an action that currently isn't our default behavior.

There are two unproductive approaches to changing your habits: beat yourself up over not having the good habit already and keep having the bad habit. In both cases, you have to catch yourself when taking the wrong approach and stop.

No excuses. No browbeating. No backsliding. No overanalysis. No delay. Right now, in this moment, have the good habit instead of the bad. When you fail, well, that wasn't it; next moment, have the good habit instead of the bad.

Escaping the bad-habit rut

Use the energy that leads you into the bad habit as fuel to carry you into another and more satisfying action. Jinx McCombs suggests envisioning what you will do in place of the bad habit and choosing something physically incompatible with what you're trying to stop doing. The new alternative should be specific, not general, so your habit-driven brain doesn't have to do any work in order to jump out of your current rut.

For example, when you find yourself biting your fingernails yet again, stop and do the alternative on which you've decided: perhaps put lotion on your hands, sharpen a pencil, or practice a sleight-of-hand coin trick. Bad habits are often a way of expressing energy, so give that energy somewhere to flow that isn't fighting against your goals.

Just get moving

Want to get fit? Stampede right over that wussy, whiny inner voice when it is saying, "Oh, I dunno. We don't really *have* to go for a walk, *do* we?" or "Okay. Five blocks is enough, *right?*"

I'm not talking about the voice of your injured knee or something like that; I mean the inner grub that just wants to sit on the couch, wiggling its tail at the TV and shoving nachos into its maw. Don't give in to it. Walk an extra 10 blocks before lunch. It won't take long at all, and it's good to shake a leg. While you're at it, tell the grub to shut up and choose something healthy for lunch that won't throw you into an afternoon food coma. Once you get moving you'll remember that you actually enjoy it, even if sometimes it's only for that sense of accomplishment.

Changing food habits

Want to eat healthier? Stop your hand as it is about to pick up some junk food and put it in your shopping cart. If you're trying to change the habit of gaining weight, here's the deal: Take in fewer calories than you burn. Two methods, therefore, are best in combination: eat less and exercise more. There is no negotiating out of that principle. You can eat lower calorie foods in the same quantity or eat high-calorie foods in smaller quantities. You can do more intense activity when you exercise or you can do lower intensity activity longer or more often.

There is no trick about shifting habits. Except—aha!—the same ideas that work for Discardia elsewhere also apply here. You don't have to change everything all at once; you just have to start changing things in the right direction more often than in the wrong.

If you're trying to lose weight, having less of a caloric overflow is still better than no reduction at all. Making sure that you walk 6,000 steps a day instead of 4,000 is better than no improvement. Aim for 10,000, but don't give up if you don't get there right away.

All this can be adapted for those who need to gain instead of lose weight, of course. Switch to a healthy, high-calorie substitute for something you currently and regularly eat, for example. Incorporating higher fat accompaniments to your meals, such as nuts, avocados, and cheeses, could help tilt the scale in the direction you want to be heading.

———

Watch for ways to set yourself up for success. Review the snacks you keep on hand around the house and at work. Do they help or harm your overall health goals? I've learned that if there aren't any corn chips or soft drinks in the house and I am limited to lower fat and less sugary snacks—like fresh baby carrots, whole grain crackers, apples, and soda water—I am just as happy and have a lot more energy.

Don't torture yourself by keeping a bunch of stuff around that you don't actually want yourself to eat. Make it easy to snack well. Try substituting smaller amounts of more intense flavors for bigger quantities of simpler foods. A wafer-thin slice of aged sharp cheddar can be nibbled for more pleasure than a hunk of some orange-dyed bland brick. A one-inch square of really good gourmet chocolate can be savored and will linger on the tongue delightfully without lingering on the hips like a Mars bar—and the darker you go, the healthier it gets! Instead of drinking a sugary, fruit-flavored drink, how about eating an actual piece of fruit and drinking a glass of water?

What you measure for is what you get

Make the big decision to do something differently—to change a habit—and then manifest that change by repeatedly making small decisions that support the big one.

Increase your awareness of how you're doing by paying attention and keeping track. Being able to answer the question, "Did I do better with this habit this week than last week?" is the key to a gradual shift that makes a new behavior stick.

Sites like the online game HealthMonth can be a huge help with recordkeeping and motivation. You can see in your log that, if you make the right choice with the current little decision, it will tip you over the line to having done better this week than last. It's a great way to break through and stop delaying on doing the right thing.

The antidotes to foolish tricks

Look around for dumb stuff you do that creates chaos in your life. Find your bad habits and build better alternatives. Here are a few examples.

———

- *Foolish trick*: Pile your plate full of too much food and then think you need to eat all of it.

- *Antidote*: Switch to smaller dinner plates. Give yourself the visual pleasure of a full plate without eating so much. Eating more slowly and stopping when you're full are also good habits, but while you're acquiring them why not take the easy win?

———

- *Foolish trick*: Pants are wrinkled after the first wearing because you drop them on the floor.

- *Antidote*: Put a clothes butler rack (or chair) right where you tend to fling things and drape things that would otherwise get wrinkled neatly over it.

———

- *Foolish trick*: Give in to the urge to shop when you have no particular item in mind and when what you really need is to relax and have a sense of accomplishment and completion.

- *Antidote*: Be mindful of your actions and urges. Answer your real needs with the right solution, not a placeholder. There are lots of better (and cost-free) ways to do this than acquiring more stuff that you don't need.

- *Foolish trick*: Buy expensive stuff and then regret it.

- *Antidote*: Take your credit card out of your wallet and store it at home—or at least tape the dang thing inside a piece of paper onto which you've written pithy questions like, "Why are you buying this?" or, "Will you still be happy about this purchase in a month?"

- *Foolish trick*: When out with friends, feel smart and witty, and speak increasingly loudly in an attempt to enlighten and impress anyone nearby with your exemplary charms (which doesn't actually work).

- *Antidote*: Lean forward conspiratorially when delivering your best lines. If you really want to be intriguing, try a little subtlety.

- *Foolish trick*: When you are not at work, find yourself gnawing away at a coulda woulda shoulda set of thoughts about work.

- *Antidote*: Cut it short. Quickly, without getting distracted into reading new mail, open your email and send yourself a very concise note expressing the actions you want to take to resolve or improve the situation. Extract the constructive part from that fuss in your brain, dismiss the rest, and send that email to your working life so you can get on with the off-duty part.

- *Foolish trick*: Brood over your wrongs that happened heaven knows how many years ago, and sit there nurturing that tension like a hen on an egg.

- *Antidote*: Take one small immediate step to improve things—and I mean little and right now—then give yourself the rest of the day off from it. How about that letter, which is half practical questions about an upcoming family event and half guilt slinging? Just answer the practical part courteously, refrain from any reciprocal slinging, and let go of the rest of that noise. What about the person you think must be mad at you for some dumb thing you did months ago and whom you've been afraid to contact? Find something small you can thank them for and send a postcard, saying something like, "Found myself listening to some Chet Baker and thought of you. Thanks for introducing me to the good stuff!" Open a door you've been holding closed. If someone comes through to reconnect, great; if not, at least you aren't spending energy on worrying about it.

- *Foolish trick*: Think, "I'm creatively stagnant" as a commercial comes on in the random TV show you started watching.

- *Antidote*: Turn off the idiot box; it saps your time and your will. Think about what you want and don't want in order to improve your odds of getting it. Wouldn't an hour of progress make you happier than an hour of random TV? If you don't want your life designed around certain actions, don't design your rooms around them. Take a look and see if you've done that with TV. If you want to do more of something, grease the slope toward doing it and make it less convenient to fall into habits of distraction. Cancel that cable subscription and only pay for things you specifically desire online or on DVD. Unless "watch more movies" is your goal, reduce your Netflix membership so those red envelopes don't nag you. If you haven't found yourself revitalized and your life improved by something you've watched on the TV within the last ten days, find a better place for it than having it dominate your living room. At the very least, get a cabinet for it today so you can hide this tool until you need it.

Open your eyes to the blockades you put between you in this moment and where and who you really want to be. When you see them, knock them down. Build bridges to your creative, happy self. Our time in this world is brief, so spend it where it matters to you and not where it doesn't. Whatever your habit is, find ways to make it harder to sabotage yourself.

Substitution tricks

Substitution tricks also take the form of fishing for praise and attention when what you really need is self-confidence. Mathematician and philosopher Blaise Pascal said long ago, "Vanity is so secure in the heart of man that everyone wants to be admired: even I who write this, and you who read this."

We all seek affirmation of our worth, but we need to keep an eye on how we go about it and avoid being conniving. I don't think anyone can be completely self-sufficient—even the most confident people I know feel unsure and are restored by praise or imitation or attraction. Accept your need for some admiration, and then go about getting it as honestly as you can. This is particularly important when it comes to relationships. Don't make your partner do a little dance for your love; give freely and accept graciously that which is genuine and caring.

Leverage your habits

While you wrestle with your brain's silly unproductive habits, watch for opportunities to leverage the way your mind works to make it more likely that you'll do the right thing.

Catching yourself surfing the web when your mind wanders at work? Yes, you can and perhaps should take advantage of software to block access to your problem sites after a certain number of minutes, but also consider the way your mind can be distracted *onto* the track with the right words and images.

Make a text file with your current top goals and set it to be your browser's default home page. Then, you will see it every time you open a new tab or window. Choose a desktop image that reminds and motivates you to focus. Make sure the artwork in your office energizes you and reinforces your goals. As with your physical world, optimize what you see first and frequently—what launches on startup, what's first in your dock or shortcut menus, what's in your browser toolbars—so they reinforce your priorities.

Shift your tasks based on your energy and the tools at hand. If you don't work on an actual mechanized assembly line, why act like you do? I don't think the average human is satisfied by mechanistic repetition without variation. All the ergonomic experts come around, telling us to vary our physical positions in order to prevent unduly stressing our limbs, but I think you need to vary your mental position just as much.

If you tend to have an energy slump in the early afternoon, schedule meetings or routine tasks then. If the late morning and late afternoon tend to be when your brain is ticking at high speed, that's when you should do heavier mental lifting, such as in-depth testing of a complex problem or writing that is not based on previous work.

Microbreaks and nanobreaks

When work is very stressful due to more falling onto your plate than it can hold, fend off that overwhelmed feeling by taking a moment to remind yourself of the good things in your life. Even if you can't take a full break and leave your desk, at least give yourself time to look out the window, stretch, and take a deep breath. Pulling yourself out of context with a microbreak when you feel the stress building will diffuse the tension and allow you to return to work a few seconds or minutes later with a fresh mind.

A variant on microbreaks, nanobreaks—a great enhancement to my stress-busting repertoire—are something I invented while working in a sad, beige cubicle. Stock your screen saver and a changing desktop pattern with pictures that make you happy: friends, flowers, landscapes, and other favorites. Then, when you need a little jolt of happiness, minimize your windows and discover something on your desktop to bring a smile to your face.

A second or two may not seem like it would make a difference, but it is profoundly useful, especially for any cube-dweller who doesn't have a beautiful view to use for recharging. Learn the keyboard shortcut or gesture on your system so it's even easier. Your desktop pattern (or startup screen or any other frequently seen image under your control) can en-courage you—not just jolly you up but actually create courage you can use to move toward your dreams.

11

Argh! Email!

Ahhh! Working System

> Each of us literally chooses, by his way of attending
> to things, what sort of universe he shall appear
> to himself to inhabit.
> —*William James, psychologist and philosopher*

Clearing your mind and your virtual desk

So far, we focused on cleaning up your physical surroundings, but your digital ones can be a significant source of stress, too. The principles aren't too different: Set up groupings that make subsequent actions easier, move things to the appropriate group the moment you decide what it is, and repeatedly use quick laps to knock down big or constant projects.

This section includes many tips particularly relevant to email for work as well as ideas that will help you build a better relationship with your personal email.

Email basics

First, a few basic principles (and a thank-you to Merlin Mann and others who have taught me many things about managing email):

Start your day with energy, not email. Take a moment to clear your head, jot down any lower priority loose ends that are distracting you and throw them in your inbox (physical or digital) to address later. Then, get to work on one of your three top tasks for the day.

> Devote the first 30 minutes of your day to a
> burst of progress on one of your highest priority
> projects or to the removal of specific distractions
> in order to improve your focus for the rest
> of the day.

Discard the idea that every email you get deserves some of your time. Make a quick evaluation and then either delete it, do any less than two-minute task, or add the appropriate task to your to-do list.

Be brief, if you need to answer at all. Not every email you get deserves to be answered with a correspondingly lengthy reply or, in many cases, any reply at all. Mail templates, which you can use to autoinsert frequently used responses, are huge time savers. Learn how to use them in your mail program.

Don't file; archive. Mail programs have search functions. Unless it's a category where you regularly need to retrieve the last activity (and you don't have that status in a more trusted system), or something that would be hard to capture in a search, just throw it in one big archive folder. If you are not using a powerful web-based mail service like Gmail, you will probably want to start a fresh archive folder for each year and store the ones from prior years in backup. Keeping separate and therefore smaller archives makes it faster for programs to locate search results.

Trash is your friend! Delete anything that requires no action on your part and isn't something you need to reference soon or in the future.

Give up your role as unnecessary mail hoarder. If this email isn't the very first place you'd look for this information, don't carefully save it for future reference. Put the information where you will look (if it isn't already there).

Stop the distraction machine. Turn off all new mail alerts. No sounds, no counts, no pop-ups. Check email on your terms, as needed, and only between doing other actions.

Filter where possible. If you know that mail fitting a particular pattern belongs to a particular task—for example, email newsletters that fit within your recurring "professional reading" activity—automatically route it to a folder for that task. Then, remove its "unread mail" status on the way there, so you aren't tempted to pay it more attention than it deserves. You'll track the need to do the recurring activity of examining those folders in your to-do's or calendar.

Finally, and most importantly: Don't use your inbox as your to-do list. It is ill suited to that purpose because it doesn't help you focus on doing. It is poor at distinguishing between things to which you want to pay attention today and things you may not need to act on for days or even weeks. You can think of your inbox as your hand, reaching out to someone who is handing you a piece of paper. Glance at the paper to see if it's urgent, but don't stand there with hundreds of pages in your hand. Instead, put the pages where they need to be. They represent actions that you will either do now, add to your to-do list, or archive. A small percentage may need to stick around briefly—with a label, as described below—but you can delete or archive pretty much everything.

Getting more out of Gmail's Priority Inbox

Gmail now offers a feature called Priority Inbox, which allows you to have up to four tiers in your email inbox with automatically detected (and adjustable) messages sorted into ranked sections. This tool is very useful and worth calling out specifically, hoping that other mail programs will add similar features. I've given it a try and find that it does help me prioritize my time better.

When I began using it, the default tiers were "Important," "Starred," and "Everything Else"; since I don't use stars that much and do have an email-intensive volunteer project, I've taken advantage of the customization options to have one section contain all the things in my inbox that have a particular label identifying them as part of that project. When I'm not working on that volunteer activity, I can minimize that section and focus on my personal mail.

I set up another section to hold everything with my "discuss with Joe" label. I also keep that minimized except when reviewing those items with my other half. If you use Gmail, I think you'll like this option, which you can turn on in the "Inbox" tab of "Mail settings." Beyond this specific tool, though, there are some great principles at work.

Principles behind a low-stress workspace

Chunk stuff together. It's easier to tackle similar items than dissimilar items. Put all those "add to calendar" notes in one group and all those "bills to confirm and pay" in another. You'll complete the tasks faster if you don't have to keep mentally switching modes from calendar to bill pay.

Isolate large projects. This is the same principle as "chunk stuff together," but it has extra benefits with longer, more focused work. Being able to close off the "hot but not necessarily strategic" and "noisy but low priority" items from your view when you are working on a project is a huge help in making effective use of that time. Whether it's the ability to sit at your desk with only that project folder in front of you and no other papers nagging at the corners of your vision, or using a software feature like the "Focused" view in OmniFocus, build yourself clear thinking space.

Enjoy your finite attention. You are going to receive more demands upon your attention than you have time for. You will get too much email and, by all kinds of methods online and off, you'll find out about too many cool links and shows and books and hobbies and ideas for anyone to explore in one lifetime. Embrace this. If you're walking on the beach and pick up every shell you see, it will impair—not increase—your enjoyment. Pass things by without anxiety. In other words, delete, archive, recycle, and unsubscribe. Don't let things pile up in the hope that you can get to them someday. Let the chaff go; heck, let a lot of the grain go. There will be more good stuff to capture your attention tomorrow.

Let everything else beyond "important" and your big projects offer itself for your consideration and then ruthlessly respond to almost none of it. Either it matters now, belongs to a project (active or inactive or new), belongs in cold storage in your someday-maybe list for later consideration, or you don't need it at all.

When feeling overwhelmed, check to see if you're considering too much stuff. Picture the intangible as physical, and the silliness of what you've been asking yourself to do will often give you the lift you need to take better care of yourself. If those 2,327 things in your inbox were pieces of paper you were trying to hold in your hands, of course you'd be stressed! Decide to do it—and manage it with your current active or inactive projects accordingly—or let it go.

Fast sorting for a calmer relationship with your inbox

Sorting incoming email faster is one of the critical ingredients of email mastery. You need to be able to process the contents of your inbox without getting bogged down and doing everything. First, know what you have. Second, do the right next thing. Take as few seconds per message as possible, and whip through your inbox and delete, file or label everything as appropriate. If you don't already have labels set up for your mail and your email program supports them, do that quickly now. Gmail, Thunderbird, and the Mac's Mail application allow you to label. You can achieve a similar effect with categories in Outlook.

You need very few labels:

"active project support" (or *"task support,"* if you prefer a shorter term). You need these emails in order to perform tasks for a current active project. If you won't do the task in the next 48 hours and you can easily copy the information in the email to your to-do list entry for that task, archive or file the email. If the task is coming up quickly, just apply the label and spare yourself the extra effort. Strike a good balance between the pleasure of an empty inbox and busywork copying information more than is necessary.

"waiting for." Use this label as a reminder of something you may need to nudge someone else later to resolve (for example, the receipt for an online order, which you will want to reference if the goods haven't arrived as expected) or for something that is queued up behind another task you expect to finish shortly.

"discuss with ___." If you regularly need to consult with someone else—your boss, perhaps, or your spouse—before deciding how to han-

dle an email, you may want to add a label so that you can easily bring up your complete list of open questions when you meet with that person.

"to read." You will probably want more than one of these (for example, *"to read: business"* and *"to read: personal"*). This label goes on anything that you can tell right away you don't need to read right now but will need to look through at some point. Catching up on these categories can be a good task when you are feeling brain dead or have only a few minutes before you go into a meeting. Periodically review your "to read" items to make sure that what once went into that bucket is still something you'd put in there today.

There can be deeper forces at work here than you might expect. We change over time, but we often experience a lag in acknowledging that change, particularly where our aspirations are involved. We hold onto expectations of what we should know and objects we thought would bring us to that state of competence. It can be curiously as difficult for us to let go of something we thought we should study as to drop a project that no longer serves our current bigger picture goals. That reluctance shows up in the language we use about managing our reading lists — biting the bullet, purging, weeding, culling — painting a picture of us killing off something alive.

As a mental exercise, consider a different metaphor next time you look at your "to read" pile: "Does this train go to the station I'm trying to reach?" Just because you don't decide to take it, the train doesn't vanish from the world or cease to be useful to other people. Let it go if it's not the one you need.

———

Bloggers may also find it handy to have a *"to post"* label for email to which they want to respond publicly or which inspires a post. In general, though, the four labels above should be sufficient to cover anything worth keeping in the inbox temporarily. If you do add more labels, consider putting a distinctive character at the start of these key ones (e.g., *"@waiting for"* or *"_waiting for"*) to insure that they are always sorted to the top of the list for quick access.

Why label instead of moving to folders? It avoids the risk of "out of sight, out of mind" while allowing you to tell at a glance that you've already handled everything that currently needs handling. You get the benefit of inbox zero without wasting a lot of time or having to establish new rituals to check special folders.

For categories of which you don't want to be reminded until you're performing a round of that activity (for example, something like, *"to read: professional development"*), folders or their equivalent are helpful. In Gmail, you can keep those pending things labeled appropriately and archived, always retrievable by selecting all messages with that label, which you remove from each one after reading it. Wherever possible I also encourage you to take advantage of any controls for showing and hiding the list of labels, which allow you to keep only your primary ones in constant view.

Remember: When processing new email, you want to be incredibly quick, spending as few seconds on each message as is necessary to answer the questions, "Does this require any action on my part?" and, if so, "What?"

GTD?

Those questions may sound familiar because they're a core part of David Allen's "Getting Things Done" approach, which I highly recommend as a source of tools for your toolbox. This approach emphasizes the importance of ubiquitous capture to get things out of your head and into a single, trusted system. It doesn't matter whether that system is paper or electronic; it does matter that you use it and you trust it. GTD advises using as few inboxes as will work for you to hold things about which you haven't yet decided and to process those inboxes at least once a day to answer the question, "Is any action required from me on this?" for each item.

> Another essential part of the GTD approach is
> to conduct a weekly review to clear your mind,
> regain perspective, and check up on all your
> active projects. Less frequent reviews should also
> be done to stay in touch with your bigger picture.
> (You'll encounter my version of a big review in
> the section on taking a stress-free vacation in
> "Symptom #24: Rushing" in Part Three.)

GTD coaches and I agree that even 45 minutes a week of pulling back to review where you stand and where you want to be heading will create a radical upswing in your ability to react constructively throughout the rest of your time.

Software supporting GTD techniques continues to proliferate and improve. I use OmniFocus on the Mac, but there are also GTD plugins for software, such as Outlook and Lotus Notes. Whatever your software environment, it's worth reading *Getting Things Done*, trying out at least some of the techniques it promotes, and searching online to see if there are ways to integrate it into the tools you already use.

Email sorting in action

You can immediately delete most email (or throw it into a single archive). My approach (using Gmail) is to scan over the unread subject lines, check the boxes for anything that you can archive without opening (for example, "John Doe is now following you on Twitter"), and click "Archive."

Then, if I saw any spam on the first pass (mercifully rare now thanks to better filters built into good mail applications), I rescan (faster this time because I've already read the subjects once), check the boxes, and click "Report Spam" to clear those out of my way.

I deal with the remaining items one by one, reading enough to determine the appropriate action. That action could be noting a task or future event by copying information to my to-do list or calendar (deferring); forwarding the message with brief comments and usually an improved subject line to someone else, if appropriate (in other words, delegating); replying, if it will take less than two minutes (doing); or labeling, if I need to keep the email for the moment to support a future task, including any responses that would take more than two minutes (again, deferring).

The goal of the two-minute "doing" limit is to avoid duplicating efforts on low-return tasks. You've spent enough energy and time to decide the necessary action so, rather than having to remind yourself again later, do the fast actions now.

Beware that the "it'll just take five or 10 minutes" emails really add up. Be firm with yourself about the two-minute limit and come back to the longer tasks after you've finished processing. Know what you have, and do the right next item instead of the one that happens to be next in your inbox.

> Building this habit into your daily routine will change your relationship with email. Instead of a murky pit of unknown obligations, your inbox will be a functional space. Repeatedly throughout your day you will know exactly what's there, if anything, and what commitments it represents when it isn't empty.

Handling old email

I hear some of you crying, "All these best practices are well and good, but what do I do with the email backlog that is clogging up my inbox?" I assure you that you don't need to deal with all of it at once. You can get rid of it—and quickly—but it will take three steps.

1. **Draw a line in the sand.** Create a label called "Old Inbox" and apply this label to everything older than 48 hours. Give it a color you dislike so you'll be motivated to get rid of that stuff. (If your mail program doesn't have labels, then drag everything to a new folder

called "Old Inbox," but you will need to be tough on yourself to keep dealing with its contents until it's empty.)

2. **Above the line, practice good inbox habits as described above.** Get clean and clear about everything in the inbox that's newer than the "Old Inbox" label. Live above the line and use search to dig for things below it only if needed.

3. **In just 10 minutes at a time, knock the old stuff into shape.** Whenever you can spare the time—but at least once a day—set a timer for 10 minutes and process the old stuff following the same good habits you're doing above the line. Do not let yourself get distracted in that time. It's just 10 minutes. You can do this! The best part? It turns out that it doesn't take very long to get through the old stuff, even if you have hundreds or even thousands of "Old Inbox" messages. Make use of the ability to sort by sender or subject to help you knock chunks of messages into the right place quickly.

———

Mastering your inbox will reduce your stress, help focus your time on the most important actions, and give you the ability to respond thoughtfully when response is appropriate. The calm and control it creates can transform the way others perceive you, building trust and respect.

More email and inbox tips

Before we leave the topic of email and inboxes, here are a few high-level tips.

Hoard your attention. It is vital that you take control over distracting default settings. There is tremendous value in turning off all audio and visual alerts to the arrival of new mail. You're not dead, so of course you have new mail or you will shortly. Unless your job is purely to read email and do nothing else that takes longer than a minute, you should not let your email flow dictate your day. If that is your job, your email is already open anyhow and you'll see the new mail arriving. Turn off the alerts.

Work on your priorities, not on what's freshest. Don't press the "Check Mail" button like a lab rat hoping to get a tasty food pellet. Yes, okay, you might get something you can answer quickly and scratch off as done, but that will not be as important as what is currently on the top of your to-do list. Do what you already spent time and energy deciding was most important. Dive in, knock out a task appropriate to your current resources and energy level, then surface and check email quickly before diving in again on the next prioritized task. By "quickly," I mean "processing." For anything that generates a new task for your list, only ask the question, "Is this more important than what I was planning to do next?" If the answer is no, which it usually is, carry on as planned. Merlin Mann said it beautifully: "Don't let the blur of movement try to replace one elegantly completed task."

Pay for checking email. If you find yourself checking mail far more often than actually results in a change in your plan of action, start forcing yourself to complete the next task on your list before you are allowed to check again. Quit the mail program if you need to keep yourself from auto-piloting back into your inbox. The task list—whatever you use to track the next steps for your projects and other high priority work—is where you need to land whenever you're not sure what comes next.

Set a good example. As you want your email processing to be quick and inspire clarity, so do those who receive email from you. Write good email. Be brief. Use good subject lines. For example, don't title it, "About next week's meeting"; instead, write, "Tuesday 8/18 ABC meeting agenda & goals." As customer experience consultant Mark Hurst suggested in his book Bit Literacy, "frontload" your messages to state the one key piece of information right up front; then, only if needed, write more to support it. The way you craft your messages can help steer the recipient to the action you want them to take.

Present the right calling card. Your email signature file identifies you and your context. People will use it to reach you and to form an opinion of you. Take a minute to be sure that it is without errors, is up to date including only the contact methods by which you want to be contacted, emphasizes what you want to emphasize, is succinct, and is text-only. Good email manners go a long way to set you apart from the crowd.

———

Email can be a huge source of stress, so time spent learning how to manage it better and putting systems and settings in place to reduce its annoyances will yield big rewards.

12

The Museum of Me

Preserve the Context, Not the Object

> Being organized does not mean buying more plastic
> boxes; being organized means you kind of only
> need this one box 'cause you only save cool stuff.
> —*Merlin Mann*

The Museum of Me

Now that your digital ducks are in a row and you can breathe a little easier, it's time to tackle some emotionally tougher stuff. It often isn't easy to decide the fate of the things our past selves have acquired. We change. We all know that's true but, when it comes to our belongings, it can be difficult to let go of our old ideas about ourselves and the accessories that supported that personality.

Psychologist and hoarding expert Dr. Randy Frost identifies this worry as being at the core of holding onto things we don't need anymore. "What am I without my stuff? What's happened over the years is the stuff has somehow invaded your sense of self, your identity, because without it you feel like you don't know who you are."

Over time, our homes (and closets and storage units) become museums to who we've been. Instead of sliding our fresh selves into the world and leaving our old snakeskins behind, we retain every one, acting as both collector and specimen. We run our own fan clubs. The San Francisco haulage program RecycleMyJunk.com tweaked this sentiment delightfully with signs on their trucks reading, "The Smithsonian already has one."

Our attachment to physical objects is tightly related to what behavioral scientists call the "endowment effect"; in other words, just owning something makes us less inclined to consider getting rid of it. However, recent studies by Stanford University and University of Pennsylvania psychologists, as cited by Katharine Sanderson in *Nature News*, have shown that the pain of parting does not derive from overvaluing the item but is pure aversion to losing something regardless of its current utility to us. Our brains get hooked on having things.

When those things are associated with memories that we don't want to lose, it becomes even harder to overcome this physical barrier to letting go of an object. Being conscious of this fact can make it easier for us to separate the thing from the memory and preserve only what truly still adds value to our lives. As reported in *Science Daily*, social psychologists at the University of New Hampshire have demonstrated that those who feel more accepted and loved by others place a lower monetary value on their possessions. As we mature and derive less of our sense of personal security from objects and more from our selves and our relationships, we gain both resilience and freedom.

As we conquer habits of acquisition and hoarding, there is no reason that we can't preserve our sense of self—and of a self that is changing over time—while also making our day-to-day lives happier and more convenient. In this digital age you can make the playlist representing the autobiographical history of music in your life instead of keeping your old vinyl records long after the last turntable has left your home. You don't have to keep the thing; you can keep the pointer to the thing, the memory, the *context*.

What matters is what matters. Always consider whether you need to keep the thing or just the emotion or attention that you bring to it. When it no longer matters, *let it go*.

You can capture context, stories, and memories in easily searchable, storable, shareable, and mobile ways that do not clutter your daily life. Whenever you can effectively represent something physical in your world by something digital, let the physical thing go. For example, you probably have a lot of flat physical objects around your home, or saved in file drawers or boxes, which have sentimental value but which you don't actually want to have on your walls. Posters or flyers from shows you attended, rough sketches, holiday picture cards from friends, etc., can pile up.

You do not need to keep a physical archive of every significant image that comes into your life. You may want to look at things later, though. You can take a picture, back up the digital copy, and get rid of paper stacks. On Flickr (and on most photo sites), it is easy to collect things into sets. You can even get a little book printed with those images. A stack of every drawing your kid made this year might be a bit much to keep, but a yearbook of your favorites along with other photos of your kid from that time might be one of the most wonderful souvenirs you have. You can supplement this with a rotating art show. Get one of those easy-to-open box frames. You'll be able to add in new pieces stacked up in front of the older pieces and keep the originals of your favorites—up to a manageable point.

Condense all that stuff into the essence of what you value about it.

Suiting to yourself now

Nurse and counselor Julie Lanoie told a sweet story in her *Downsize Challenge* blog. Her elderly grandfather had several old suits—now never worn—that a lifelong friend personally tailored for him years ago. She had one of them made into a shoulder bag he can use every day to keep track of the few things he currently needs to carry. Lanoie asked her readers the great question, "What could you do with the beloved things that no longer suit you in their current form?" When I shared this story in the Discardian Facebook community, member Ellen Scott Grable told us that she turns her old cashmere sweaters into throw pillows and gives them as enthusiastically received gifts.

Do you want to be the archivist of this?

When it comes to family memories, as a genealogist I understand the import of keeping old photos; however, if they have no indication of who they are—and believe me, we've found many photos of friends and neighbors to whom we are not related among the past century of old family pictures—they are going to be of limited use. Definitely try to find a home within the family, take a good digital photo of the original picture and circulate it by email to all who you think *might* be related and let someone claim the original (or perhaps identify the subjects, which might change your feelings for it), but you are not required to hold onto things for posterity.

That's a controversial position, I know, but if you don't want to maintain the family archive, let that fact be known so someone who does actively engage with these items and feels an obligation to them can take them. Most families have people on both ends of this spectrum. If you don't really care about these objects, you're not going to take great care of them, so get them to a more appropriate home. If no one in your family wants them, or you're the last of your line (as I am on my father's side), you can offer them out to the wider world. It's getting easier and easier to take a look on Geni.com, Ancestry.com, or similar sites and see if you can find some distant cousin who'll be thrilled to get a box of old photos or letters for their genealogy project.

Digitally preserving your memory

Memories are easier to digitize than you might think. Start a blog (well-established hosted services like TypePad and Blogger are very good) and write about why the object matters to you and of what it reminds you. Take digital photos or scan flat things, and put the pictures and the stories up on your website. My friend, software engineer and program manager Lilly Tao, did a great project like this for all her old t-shirts. By putting souvenirs online, it is easy to remember something as well as share stories with friends and family.

If web publishing isn't quite your style, gather some friends and tell your stories as a way of bidding things farewell. You may find that it often isn't the physical souvenir itself that holds the importance of the story. Get together for a low-key show-and-tell brunch and share the stories of your things, and then have everyone hop in the car and donate all these items you've honored. You'll help others, learn more about your friends, and freshen those favorite old memories while clearing space in your home for your present and future life.

Telling these stories and then letting go can work very well in combination with a project like Discardian Erin Hare's "31 Things Out of the

____" sprint on basements, attics, etc., or designer Randy Reddig's "Less 365." Whether you let go by the month or the year, say farewell to some physical encumbrances and acknowledge your journey so far.

Consider digitizing the things you have on display in your home. If your house should ever suffer damage, it's nice to know that you have a backup digital copy as well as one you can easily access on the web. Of course, you can do this with little tchotchkes, too. Don't really want to keep that epic collection of refrigerator magnets, but want to remember the glory days when it covered the entire front surface of your fridge? Take some photos, maybe keep a handful of favorites, and sell the rest at your next yard sale. (Just don't set the bag of 'em next to the hard drive where you have all those backups, okay?) Take this approach with any physical stuff that is more about the emotion than the thing.

Collections and change

Got a whole lot of one kind of thing? What if 90% of that collection went away? Purge that which accumulates by habit—clipped articles, mugs, fancy condiments—but which you wouldn't replace if starting fresh today. Examine those masses of things you keep that all go together and see how many of the set you still use or enjoy.

The waffle irons of our souls

Before we move on, let's take note of some things that may not at first glance seem to be part of the "Museum of Me" but that definitely hold an emotional load, making it harder to part with them.

Writing can have a profound impact upon us. Essayist Joseph Epstein said, "Reading is experience. A biography of any literary person ought to deal at length with what he read and when, for in some sense, we are what we read."

Add to this the similarly shaping powers of music and film. We cling to the physical shells of these formative experiences—books, CDs, videos—as though they were pieces of our identity itself. We even do this with media which we we do not intend to re-experience anytime soon, if ever.

If you're not going to reread that book every few years, isn't there a less space-invasive way to represent your life history as a reader than keeping it? If you never put on that music but prefer instead to have it randomly appear in your life—on the radio, perhaps, or playing in a store—then why keep a copy of it when someone else could enjoy that copy? If you aren't inclined to watch that movie again for a decade or so, why keep it in its current form when movie formats have changed at such a rapid pace in the last 20 years? It is the experiences—not the objects—that we are trying to preserve. Tell your stories. Acknowledge your influences. Let your old snakeskins go.

The big impermanence

The last and biggest fallacy of maintaining the "Museum of Me" is the notion that your body will serve you some purpose after you die.

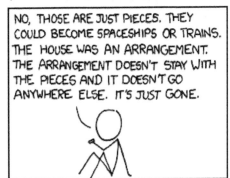

Illustration by Randall Munroe, xkcd. Used by blanket permission.
[Mouseover text: "Dad, where is Grandpa right now?"]

Identify yourself as an organ donor and let your family know that you want to have your body parts distributed to someone who needs them after you die. Learn more at organdonor.gov or search for a similar resource in your country if you're outside the United States.

Think and talk about your preferences in life and death. As Dr. Atul Gawande reported in his 2010 article "Letting Go: What Should Medicine Do When It Can't Save Your Life?" in the *New Yorker*, "People have concerns besides simply prolonging their lives. Surveys of patients with terminal illness find that their top priorities include, in addition to avoiding suffering, being with family, having the touch of others, being mentally aware, and not becoming a burden to others."

It's a somber thing to think about, but as you progress with Discardia and identify more of those things in life that contribute most to your happiness, give some thought to how you do and don't want to bring down the curtain at the end. Make sure your family knows your preferences.

Your time in this world is the real treasure.

13

But I Should Want This

Who Would Really Appreciate This?

> When the last kid to sleep in the baby bed drives the
> car to Goodwill, you know it's an overdue disposal.
> — *Steve Yelvington, new media strategist
> and disruptive influence*

Old toys

We're so used to infusing our things with emotional significance that sometimes we react to objects as though they were *supposed* to be important to us. It is more than possible that they aren't important at all. A good example are old toys, which no one—you, the kids, the cat, or whoever—plays with anymore because they're broken, dirty, or simply boring. Old toys are digested remnants of past fun. Some of them wouldn't be fun for anyone now and can go in the trash. Boring ones can go in your charity box. Put them in there as soon as you think, "I don't really want this anymore."

Maybe you feel guilty about getting rid of that perfectly good toy you no longer like. *Stop.* It may be perfectly good for someone, but that someone isn't you. There's nothing inherently wrong with getting rid of it. Who are you worried about offending? Just ask, "Who would really appreciate this?" If the answer is "Me," then keep it; otherwise, send it on to a better home with good wishes.

The best way to ensure that a thing you no longer want ends up in the right hands is to donate it to someone who reaches more people than you do. The Goodwill donation bin does more good than the combination of the back of your closet and your best intentions. If you have guilt over getting rid of things, relieve it by slowing the incoming flow. Buy fewer or better things that will last and be satisfying to you for longer.

Pay attention to your payoff:effort ratio

Decide what your time is worth and quit (or phase out) what generates losses in money, time, or joy. For example, I rarely use coupons (they're too much hassle for far too little return), do not keep or carry pennies (the monetary value does not exceed the pleasure of lighter pockets and purse), and generally do not shop at warehouse stores (lower prices do not compensate for poorer selection, inconvenient location, and dumb impulse buys).

Rejects can be rewards

Every now and then, you'll find an unexpected case where you really appreciate some neglected object. Go shopping in the back of your closets, basement, attic, or other cold storage spots. You'll unearth stuff to toss, but I bet you'll find at least one happy surprise, too. Weed out the unwanted and see what you uncover!

Your rejects can be rewards to others. Still have the digital camera you bought before the one you bought before your current one? Send those old ones to a friend or relative who needs an upgrade. Giving a digital camera to a kid can be an especially great gift, opening up their creative world. That's a much better fate than having it collect dust at your place.

Whether it's someone you know or charity recipients, let go of something that will make other people happy. More often than not, the combination of clearing stale stuff from your life and the pleasure of creating happiness are the big profits you will gain from Discardian projects. Consider that payoff when you're debating whether the hassle of trying to sell old things is worthwhile. Do not get hung up justifying the fate of things you discard. As author Matthew Amster-Burton said, "You don't have to be responsible for making sure all of your former stuff reaches its proper place in the universe."

If it's not right for you now, get rid of it. Give yourself the payoff of having it gone without worrying about whether you should have found a new home for it or made money selling it. Think of it this way: Goodwill is like a spa where things relax before they move to a new home.

———

Let go of sunk costs and take the rewards inherent in having less of the wrong stuff in your way.

Hounded by Worry and Fear

14

SOLUTION

Take Your Chances and Cut Your Losses

> Your brain produces thoughts in a stream of
> narrative just like—and I'm going to use an awful
> simile here, but it's apt—just like your intestines
> produce excrement. You've got a lot of crap in your
> head and most of it isn't true.
> —*Martha Beck, sociologist and therapist*

Emotions are real, but dangers may not be

Fear can stand between you and a life in which you'd be happier. If you fear change, it can be a lot harder to let go of things. When you're feeling resistance about your life being different, try personifying your fear. Imagine a little scaredy-cat person about three feet tall, with perky ears and a cute black spot over one eye. Picture yourself showing it the better possibility that it is reluctant to approach, and take a good look at what it is clinging to instead. Calm it down, pick it up, and carry it gently forward to where you want to go.

"See? It's not so bad."

You probably won't turn it into a brave, change-loving, life-optimizing adventure cat right away, but that's fine. Acknowledge that the feelings are real, even if the dangers aren't.

Only fight the real battles

Faced with an area of your life that seems to lure you into frequent worrying? Watch out for worrying about multiple incompatible outcomes and thinking you'll need to have the strength to weather them all. The best way to get yourself through future hardship is not to make yourself a wreck right now. Have the conversation that tests the factual basis for your fears. Spend your mental energy working on solving real—not imaginary—issues.

For each worry, find one small tangible thing you can do to make it less likely or less harmful should it become real. Remember that you don't have to solve everything all at once. A step in the right direction is a good thing and better than being a deer in the headlights. Decide on a positive action and let yourself move ahead.

Don't forget to ask, "What's the problem I solved in order to have this one?"

Give yourself credit for the progress you've made.

Begin!

It's important to let yourself stop when things aren't right for you, but it's even more important to let yourself start without worrying that you have to be perfect. Why are you still sharpening your crayons when you should have already started coloring? Simply *begin*.

When there's something that you know you really want to do—and circumstances are all lined up to support it—but it's a really big leap, ask yourself if the regret from not doing it will outweigh the risks if you do. It's good to plan, have safety nets, and keep yourself from becoming overextended in general, but sometimes it is the right time to stretch. Don't avoid something just because you're afraid to fail or you're being afraid to succeed.

If a great opportunity falls in your lap but would be tricky to bring off successfully, see if there's a way you can give it a try while maintaining an escape plan. If so, set up the timeline for when you will definitely proceed with it or will use that exit. Then, go for it. When you're trying to make a project come together, be sure to weigh regularly the work required, the time remaining, and the chances for success. If the picture gets bleak, instead of exhausting yourself for a poor result, choose one of these options:

- Scale the project back to make it achievable with the originally planned amount of work in the time remaining;

- Extend the deadline to allow you to fit in more work at a non-stressful pace; or

- Decide it will not come out well enough to be worth it, cut your losses and call it off.

As time goes on you'll get better at estimating the work required, calculating the time things take, and judging before commitment whether something will be rewarding. If you let yourself intelligently make some mistakes by taking some risks, you can learn from them. Doing is how we grow. Take a fun, adventurous step outside your boring, old comfort zone.

Discarding the fears that downgrade your life

With our health, we can set ourselves up for unnecessary future hardships by neglecting preventative care now. Long overdue dealing with a health-related task? Enough! Pick up the phone, write the letter, or whatever. Quit delaying. Information makes you healthier than avoidance. Afraid of dentists? Here's the trick: Don't treat your mouth like crap and find a *good* dentist.

> If you brush twice a day and floss daily, you will you have a nice, kissable mouth and have dramatically reduced the risk of gum disease, cavities, and other ailments that make the dentist have to do painful things to you.

Some dentists and hygienists know how to make the process much less uncomfortable. They do this through a mix of strong interpersonal skills, the latest equipment, good physical techniques, and genuine care for their patients. If your dentist doesn't seem to be on your side, find one who is. Ask friends for recommendations. When you're talking to a prospective new dentist's office, ask about how they reduce the pain of common procedures, such as cleanings. You deserve to have the best care from those you hire and from yourself.

———

Here's another worry on which you can quit wasting time: Lexicographer Erin McKean of *A Dress A Day* urges women to stop worrying about being visually pleasing to everyone: "You don't owe prettiness to anyone. Not to your boyfriend/spouse/partner, not to your coworkers, especially not to random men on the street. You don't owe it to your mother, you don't owe it to your children, you don't owe it to civilization in general. Prettiness is not a rent you pay for occupying a space marked 'female'."

Likewise, men should rebel against that social pressure not to be "too" gentle or soft. Guys: It is not required that you have any interest in sports. Be yourself.

Risking to reap the big rewards

Relationships are great opportunities, but sometimes it's very scary to consider revealing your feelings and fears. You know, those parts of yourself of which you aren't so proud and those things that you have identified as the potential weak spots for keeping it all tickety-boo with this sweetheart?

This is that "terror territory" where life can get harder, things could turn out to be deal-breakers, and all kinds of uncomfortableness could arise. It's so easy and tempting to stay in the safe zone. At some point, in order to get things better and stronger and more rewarding with a partner, you must venture out of what feels pleasant and predictable. Have some deeper conversations. Share some fears. Expose some vulnerabilities. Talk about what you want, what you really really want. There are levels of intimacy you can't fall up into; you have to climb.

It's worth it.

———

Relationships aren't the only place where our fears interfere with our happiness. At work, we can hold ourselves back by undervaluing our own talents and not speaking up for what we truly want to be doing in our careers. We may underpromote ourselves and miss opportunities for advancement and growth. We may chase advancement too far trying to meet others' definition of success and neglecting our own sense of the daily work we really like best. In either case, figure out where you want to be heading and start asking for that. Don't wait for others to build your future for you.

———

Laugh away your little fears and whittle away your big ones. *Be bold!*

15

Anger, Resentment, Intolerance

Ain't No Thang

> We must learn to live together as brothers
> or perish together as fools.
> —*Martin Luther King, Jr., civil rights leader*

Getting perspective

Sometimes we have to take a time out to get perspective on what is upsetting us. Take an hour or two for yourself. Take a walk or close the door and relax in private at home. The important part is to create some solitude to think a bit.

———

Of what emotion do you keep stoking the coals out of habit but from which you are now ready to move on? Is it time to stop grieving and resume living or move on from longing for someone who isn't the one for you? Should you quit swallowing your pain and cutting someone far too much slack for the hurt they cause you? Are you still chewing on the bones of old grudges? How's that working for you? Does it give you something worthwhile?

If you're feeling angry or jealous, what would need to happen for you to let go of that upset feeling? These feelings burn up an enormous amount of energy. Who or what could you make peace with today and how would it change your life to do so? Write a letter, schedule some counseling, forgive someone or yourself, but let it go and move on.

———

Slow yourself down, look around, and see the good things for which to be thankful. Don't shout or make bitter, snarky remarks at the poor retail or service staff. As author and software engineering manager Michael Lopp, who is also well known on Twitter as Rands, said, "Relax and relate before you escalate."

Lay off the car horn; it doesn't do any good and it makes the world unpleasant. Let it slide and smile. Yes, optimize where it matters but when it doesn't, let it go by and move on sweetly. Let the rest of that dumb stuff go; aggravation is a bad investment of your time and energy anyhow.

———

Don't sweat it. Get some perspective. A lot of things that may aggravate you only do so because you have the luxury of not wrestling with bigger issues. Today, be thankful for everything you have: being alive, your friends and family, your health, a roof over your head, something to eat, clean water to drink, indoor plumbing, heating, air conditioning, clothes, shoes, a job, and freedoms. Many, many people have it worse.

Bad drivers in front of you or annoying coworkers or technical difficulties aren't that important in the grand scheme of things. Yeah, okay, they're irritating, but are they important? No, not really. In those far less common situations when it really does matter, be kind and hold your ground. Sometimes all you can give is courtesy, but it's a stronger bargaining position than combativeness.

Entrepreneur and software engineer Chris Wetherell offered precise instructions in this art: "How to be nice: (Step-1) Be. (Step-2) Be nice. (Step-3) Stop being a dick. (This last step is CRUCIAL.)"

Meditate on where you spend your emotional energy and what kind of life that is giving you. If it's not the life you want, start changing it. Right now. *Today.* Change your direction and step toward where you want to be.

Make things better

What about that thing—even that little, dumb thing you did a long time ago? Today's a good day to say you're sorry. Remember Internet humorist and programmer Greg Knauss's First Rule of Arguing: "If you're feeling defensive, it's because you know, deep down, you've done something wrong."

Make things better between you and the other person. Flowers are optional but often wildly appreciated. Write that note to rebuild a relationship. Quit beating yourself up over a past mistake; make amends and move on. Apologize for that transgression about which you've been brooding. If you don't want to dredge up old badness, make this Appreciation Day and instead be nice to that person about whom you're feeling a little guilty. This counts even when the one you've wronged was yourself. Forgive; move on.

Constructive conflict

You may never find the common ground that allows you to understand entirely why an opponent approaches the situation as he does, but you do need to let go of the idea that he does what he does because he is stupid or evil. Let go of this so you can move forward from a position of greater comprehension about the whole situation. Let go of this so that others—opponents, allies, or observers—are less inclined to see you and your viewpoint as naive. Let go of this so you are more open to a successful outcome.

Focus on words and actions, not speculations about motives and intentions. As hip-hop deejay and social commentator Jay Smooth reminded everyone in his magnificent *How to Tell People They Sound Racist* video, you want to have the "what they did" conversation and not the "what they are" conversation; the latter is too easy for your opponent to derail and escape.

While you're holding others accountable for what they say and do, keep an eye on yourself. We've all got biases. Examine them and see if they're just a bad habit that got stuck to you. What do you want to unlearn? From whom are you needlessly—and hurtfully to them and to yourself—holding yourself apart? Acknowledge others' humanity as equal to your own. Turn your feet to journey step by small step to a place where groundless bias isn't part of how you relate to the world.

Delicious diversity

Today is a good day to look around with fresh eyes at the country where you live and notice the things you love about it. Find common ground with your neighbors and with those people whom you sometimes forget are your neighbors.

For people in the United States, I offer this challenge: Appreciate the differences that make this country so vital and fascinating. That means embracing the true diversity of Bible Belt conservatives and urban liberals; new immigrants and Daughters of the American Revolution; and Spanish-speaking, fifth-generation, Californian farm workers and California's foreign-born former governor, Arnold Schwarzenegger. It's a wild and frustrating mix, difficult to blend and to understand the other viewpoints, but we can't pretend that only the parts we like exist and that the rest could be eliminated. Like a person with both pleasing and irritating habits, the pieces make the whole with which we interact. Make the best of it—and I don't mean "lump it." I mean these words very literally: Make it the best you can make it.

———

As you open your eyes to the diverse mix that creates your community—any community, even ones that, on the surface, appear homogeneous—discard your isolation from those who are different. Many European countries border on as many as 10 or more neighboring countries; the United States only borders on two. No wonder it's hard for average folks in the U.S. to afford a vacation and experience life in another country.

You can visit cultural centers within the nearest big city. Spend a weekend—or at least a whole day—in a place where people mostly speak a different language. Eat new foods, hear new sounds, and learn about the history and traditions of another culture.

Choose where to explore by finding out the other languages on your local election ballot or your library's website. Call the local library and ask about census numbers for languages spoken. Search your city name on the web and the demographics data will probably also give you interesting information (though do consider the source before you assume it's accurate).

There's a big wide world out there and the boundaries between cultures and nations are dropping all the time. We can think globally and act locally but, thanks to technological changes, we can also take more of our personal world with us around the globe.

Author and futurist Bruce Sterling described his roaming lifestyle like this: "As long as I've got broadband, I'm perfectly at ease with the fact that my position on the planet's surface is arbitrary. It's the nation-state system that is visibly stressed by these changes ... Unless I'm physically restrained by some bureaucracy, I don't think I'm going to stop this glocally nomadic life. I live on the Earth. The Earth is a planet. This fact is okay."

———

Discard your knee-jerk biases based on philosophical or spiritual affiliation. I know, I know, easier said than done, but see if you can catch yourself in the act of not listening as soon as you know that the person speaking (or writing) is a [insert belief system here]. This is particularly common across the boundary of belief and nonbelief in God (or gods). Secular humanists are very quick to tune out the religious, missing out on deep insights and traditions of charity. As many disheartening surveys in the United States still reveal, atheists are dramatically less trusted than any other groups listed, despite their significant numbers and contributions even in a highly religious country like the United States.

Try reading something across the boundaries of your beliefs. C.S. Lewis's *The Screwtape Letters* and *Mere Christianity* have something to offer even a diehard atheist. *The Selfish Gene* by Richard Dawkins, or just about anything by Carl Sagan, can help theists and deists understand the love and passion that the irreligious can bring to the world around them. If those are too big a jump, then read the humorous *Hitchhiker's Guide to the Galaxy* by atheist Douglas Adams, or enjoy Sister Wendy's books and videos on great art of the world. Learn what you can see from a viewpoint to which you've previously closed yourself off.

This also goes for politics, of course, but you guessed that, right?

Going in graciously

What about the next social occasion where you need to spend time around your ideological opposites? Rather than wasting a lot of energy building up to an encounter which you expect to be tense, go into it with an open mind and be a bit more kind yourself. Perhaps you and that relative argue every year when you see each other; maybe this time you could avoid it if you don't spend days in advance practicing your arguments in your head.

Be gracious.

Forgive.

If the other person won't melt the ice on their side, give them (and you) some distance and spare yourselves the scene.

———

Bottom line: Always stay open to the possibility that conflict can be discarded. When it feels like you're on opposite teams, it's always worth asking, "How can we both get what we want?" Most games are not zero-sum.

Haunted by the Black Dog

16

Depression Is a Liar

> [Despair] is marked by a desire to get rid of the self,
> or put another way, by an unwillingness to become
> who you fundamentally are.
> — *Gordon Marino, professor of philosophy*

You deserve better

Are you sad? Depressed? That's a tough space to escape. You can't just "make happy" or let that one go so easily. However, there are some good techniques to loosen depression's hold on you. Get active.

> Every day, spend at least half an hour walking
> or gardening or otherwise being aware of the
> surroundings outside your room and office.

Get involved. Do something regularly to help other people. Volunteer once a month at a soup kitchen or the library. Help a senior or ill person in your neighborhood with errands or groceries. Become aware of the good times. Keep a journal and be sure to write in it when times are good as well as when they're bad. Depression can make it seem like things will be bad from here on out, but depression is a liar. It helps to be able to see your cycles.

If getting up and walking out the door feels as impossible as walking through the wall, bring in a pro and see if your depression is chemical in nature. If you have a physical illness—and that's what clinical depression *is*—work with your doctor and supportive friends and family to create a treatment plan just as you would for any other ailment. You deserve not to have to put up with some hormonal imbalance making your time needlessly crappy.

More than that, *no one* should have to live a needlessly crappy life. Whether driven by your own changes or that in combination with a good prescription, take better care of yourself. You do deserve it. It can get better.

Now has its charms

On a day where the outside world is making you glum, think of the antithesis to today and its weather, and think about why you might be wishing for exactly this. Do something perfectly seasonal. When I contemplated one sad, rainy day, I looked on Twitter and found that the weather was provoking the urge for naps, soup, fires in fireplaces, and misty, fresh, damp walks, which didn't sound so bad at all. *Now* has its charms when you remember to view it from the right angle.

Let go of some tension

Go slow. Be kind, especially to yourself. Unknot your knots. Sometimes you need to lose your mood in an absorbing but not challenging project. Take an easy win. You'll break out of brooding and give yourself some positive progress of which you can feel proud.

Clutter canary in the coalmine

If you are kicking yourself about getting behind on housework, stop and think about whether you've been down in the dumps lately. For many people—and I'm certainly one of them—not having the enthusiasm or willpower to take care of their surroundings can be a warning sign that they are in a depressive spell. Try viewing clutter as a reminder to check in with yourself. Are you doing things that help you manage your mood? Avoiding stuff that can trigger your depression?

When you find yourself engaged in bad habits, take time to check in with your mood and see if you can arrange things so you're more constructive with your emotions. Instead of treating clutter (or compulsive shopping or eating junk food or whatever your personal bugbear is) as a stick with which to beat yourself, use it as one of those reflective warning markers at the side of the road, which keep you from driving into a ditch.

Getting out

One of the best things you can do for yourself when you are repeatedly down in the dumps is to discard your isolation. Make a deal with yourself that you are not going home this evening without first going out and about.

Don't go to a movie. Don't go someplace where no one talks to each other. Go to a coffeehouse that has board games and find someone to play with you. Try the senior center or chat with neighbors working in their yards. Go to a bowling alley or ice rink to ask for some help to improve your skills; a pub to improve your darts game; or the grocery store to pick a good avocado. Walk through the dog park and see if someone will let you throw a ball for their enthusiastic puppy. Visit the bookstore and ask for recommendations from other customers. Go to the coffee shop at a museum and find someone who'll take you to their favorite piece and tell you why they like it. Pretend to be a tourist and ask people to tell you the best place to hang out in your town. Do not come home until you've had at least three interesting conversations.

Even a smaller version of this will help. If the weather isn't absolutely horrid—and, if it's just sprinkling a little, you aren't excused!—pop out of the house this evening and walk about a bit. Go look at the park or head up to the nearest high ground to get a view into the distance. Stroll down to the shops and pick up some fresh bread or something nice for dinner or dessert. Look around as you walk. Make eye contact with people. Smile and greet them as you pass.

Exercise will help you out of the doldrums as well as strengthen your body, help control your weight, and thus help you live longer. Unfortunately, when you're depressed, you're also lethargic, but you don't have to go jogging for an hour to shake that off. Walk down to the end of the block. Go ahead and do it. Grab the recycling, take it down to the bin, and just keep going. Take a look around at what's happening on your street. Any new neighbors moving in? Flowers blooming in yards or windows? Kids playing? Houses getting painted? Garden gnomes? Trees budding? Animal tracks? Sleeping cats? Barking dogs? What's the exceedingly local news?

When you get to the corner, see how you feel. Maybe you'll want to go all the way around the block. If not, don't worry about it. Come home and do a little stretching inside.

> Every day, walk for 10 minutes.

Ten minutes. That we can definitely do, you and I.

Part Three

September Discardia: Core Principle #2— Quality over Quantity

Make room in your life for awesomeness

In September, let Discardia be your reminder to aim for what's ideal, in just the right amount. You've got a solid foundation. You know how to make decisions about your priorities and act on them. Now you can reap the benefits.

Carve away the clutter and polish the valuables that start to shine through. You're all warmed up, so it's time to be a hardass about making life more excellent. Any junk that has survived this far into the year needs to justify its place in your life.

When you want the whole to be better, inquire of the details "Is this necessary?"

17	SYMPTOM ## Carrying an Albatross SOLUTION ## Lighten Your Load

> Never underestimate the value of
> removing friction from your day.
> —*Michael Lopp*

Why weight?

What are you carrying around with you every day? Take your backpack, laptop bag, purse, wallet, and beltware and lay it all out on the table. Do you really need all this crud with you all the time? Do some weeding to optimize your kit. Are you using the right thing in which to carry it? Last time I did this exercise I changed to a smaller laptop bag, which set an upper ceiling on the amount of stuff that can accrete into my routine load.

Create your kits

Make a mini-kit that has only the essentials for a walk or evening out. I have a simple wallet that holds my transit passes, ATM card, credit card, paper money, health care card, and ID. With that, my keys and my smartphone (with its built-in camera), I'm pretty much ready for anything that doesn't require my computer.

If you often work on the go, create an on-the-road kit with the essentials for your productivity. Discardian freelancer Mary Hawkins shared this tip: "I recently transformed an empty makeup bag into a 'freelancer's bag.' It has everything I need to be productive in someone else's office for the day—my extra hard drive, my favorite mouse, a handful of pencils and some stickies, headphones, extra cables, cough drops, eyedrops, chapstick … Most of those things were just floating around in my bag, so now that I have everything consolidated, I can just take it [out] when I don't need it and free up a bunch of space. It's also see-through, so I know what I have with me and keep everything in it relatively neat."

Keep the core items at the ready

If you have different kits for different purposes—for example, a purse, a laptop bag, and an errand satchel—set each up with the things you always need so you only have to transfer your unique items when you head out. I move my wallet, phone, and key ring to the appropriate bag knowing that it already has a pen, handkerchief, index cards for notes, business cards, and a comb. This is one place a little redundancy makes a lot of sense.

Optimize for what you really do need often and what would be a serious hassle if you needed it and didn't have it. Then keep fine-tuning to keep up with changes. It's amazing how fast you can collect random stuff and carry it around constantly.

> Get in the habit of quickly returning your daily kit to its base condition. Toss that extra change into a jar on your dresser, throw out the bits of trash, and put the receipts in with your bills, at least once a week or, better yet, each time you get home. Your back will thank you!

Pack less, way less

You really appreciate having less when you're racing across an airport or schlepping from train to train in a strange place. Traveling with a single carry-on bag is an art form well worth mastering. Don't just figure, "Hey, the airlines let me check a bag, so I might as well do so."

You can cure yourself of this habit the first time you walk off a plane with nothing but a carry-on and are on your way, while everyone else is milling around waiting. Next time you're at the airport, watch the people claiming their luggage. I certainly hope some of them are actually moving to the country at which they're arriving because you shouldn't need a bag the size and weight of a coffee table to get you through a vacation. Who looks oppressed and in pain? Giant Bag People. Who looks excited and adventurous? The ones walking past baggage claim on their way to the exit because they already have all their reasonable amount of stuff.

I went away to a very different climate for a week and a half with a carry-on, and it was fine. In fact, I could have left behind two of the long-sleeved shirts I brought. Really, up to a point—which for me is three days' worth of underwear, socks and undershirts, plus two outfits to go over them—the less you bring, the better a vacation you'll have. If you forget something, you can get by without it, borrow it from a friend, or buy it at your destination as a souvenir and keep it on your essentials list for the next trip.

When you get back, think about what worked well and what you missed. The little changes we make to smooth our travel experience are often worth making all the time. What have you figured out that you can do without?

———

Having just the right things when you aren't home is a great place to begin having the right things—and *only* the right things—throughout your life. Take the lessons you learn on the road and apply them to your other kits—from emergency supplies to your bedside table.

Stupid simple filing

It's also possible to take a lot of weight off your mental load. Here's a shocking proposition and recommendation that could change your life (it certainly changed mine): Practice stupid simple filing to manage any papers you keep. Many people procrastinate on filing; in fact, most dread it. Here's my theory: It is because most filing systems suck. They are painfully overcomplex and inefficient.

Folks like David Allen have suggested ways to make this less awful. Use a simple A-Z order. Only when needed, make separate folders for specific things (e.g., an Insurance folder behind the general "I" folder). Most importantly, keep way fewer things. You can also make the filing process less unpleasant by using pretty folders and nicer filing cabinets and fancy labels and ... ah, screw it. Filing is dull and uninspiring. I'll tell you how I do it.

Arrange to receive in digital form (rather than on paper) things you do not routinely need to access. Bank statements are a great example of the kind of thing that you can later get online in the rare case you need it.

Keep only papers you have high confidence you'll need again or that the government requires you to keep or that it stresses you out to think about discarding or shredding at this moment.

Make as few folders as possible for your comfort. Yes, A–Z, but also make folders for the stuff you know you'll have a bunch of (e.g., Next Year's Tax Prep) or will need in a hurry or when stressed (e.g., Homeowner's or Renter's Insurance, Health Insurance, Automotive Repair). This amount of filing doesn't take a lot of space and you might be able to get by with one of those clever storage ottomans with hanging file rails inside it.

Make a folder called Manuals and throw the booklets for new stuff you acquire in there. Add warranty info and purchase receipts for major things until they expire. I like to put the newest thing at the front of the folder, and weed it out once a year or so to purge papers for stuff I discarded without sending the manual along with the item.

Put everything else you think you have to keep in one stack. Seriously, just stack it up. Make it very handy to add to the stack and very unoffensive to your eye. My rule is "one neat pile of limited height or else it's gone or filed (in the A–Z files in the cabinet)." Too big a stack (say, over a foot) and you won't be able to find the things you need quickly enough. More than one stack and you won't get the benefit of knowing exactly where to look.

My stack sat on an upper shelf above eye level when I had a seated desk; now, it resides behind two more constantly used desk items below eye level at my treadmill desk. If I happen to spot a beautiful 9x12 open-topped box, I might incorporate it, but so far it hasn't been necessary. Eco-blogger Julie G of *Go Greener Australia* has had a similar experience.

She sorts through her stack once a year at tax time and hasn't found that, even after four years of this approach, she has had to clear out the file cabinet.

Using stupid simple filing, I have discovered that I spend far less time flipping quickly down through the reverse chronological stack to find one of the few things I actually wind up needing than I ever spent filing, so why file?

When the pile gets unappealingly high (or reaches one foot, whichever comes first), whip through it quickly and pull out obviously stale stuff that you can now discard or shred, or for which you have since created a file folder because you turned out to need those papers all together very often.

Here's the really sneaky part: Since you know that you'll be adding to it again soon, you are not required to completely file or discard everything in the stack. If you feel anxious about what to do with it, just leave it on the bottom and deal with it next time when it's less emotionally loaded or uncertain.

Is it perfectly orderly? No. Do I know right where to look for something when I turn out to need it? Yes.

Less time filing = more time for working on things that really matter to me!

———

Keep an eye open for those places where you're burdening yourself unnecessarily and then shed most of that needless weight.

18

But I Might Need It Someday

Someday Is Now

> It's reduce-reuse-recycle, not refuse-regret-repeat.
> —*Tiana Thomas, Discardian*

"Just in case" crowds out present opportunities

Traveling in the 21st century continually reminds us of how much we have in common with people in other places. I've been able to pop into a corner store for some forgotten item in cities from Nairobi to Nara to Newcastle. If that's true while traveling most places on the globe, it's even truer in your hometown. Quit hanging onto so much stuff "just in case." Come on. You aren't on the moon! Let the excess go.

Right now, set down the book and go recycle all but one each of your recyclable "useful" hoardings, such as glass jars and paper sacks. Trash the trash. You do not need 80 rubber bands.

Start now

Find it a little daunting to think of going through all the stuff you've saved? It won't be any easier decades from now or for someone else to do it. Discardian Diane Christeson shared her experience with this challenge in the Discardia Facebook community: "This is my year for Discardia. I turned sixty, and after some inner debate about how to mark the event, I decided to accept myself—to dump the negative attitudes I've held about myself for too many years. And my mother died. I had to clean out her house; she and Dad had lived there 31 years, and I can't count the times I heard 'It might come in handy,' and 'It'll be more expensive later, so we stock up,' and the like. Because their house is 400 miles from mine, it took me four months to clear out more than 50 cubic yards of junk and extraneous useless stuff. And that doesn't include what went to family, friends and charity. Since I recovered from that task, I've been on a crusade to clear out the extraneous and useless from my and my husband's home and lives. Feels great!"

———

Fifty cubic yards? What a task! It's far better not to have to do it all at once. Let's start with something smaller; give your medicine cabinet an emetic. Purge it of all no-longer-recommended home remedies (including everyone's favorite: ipecac syrup), expired medications, beauty products you know you'll never use and any other useless crap clogging up your shelves.

Note that prescription drugs—especially antibiotics, hormone medications, and antidepressants—should never be flushed down the toilet because modern treatment facilities are not designed to remove those medications. You can minimize their impact on the environment by taking all your unwanted or expired medicines to an appropriate disposal facility. Find their locations by calling your local pharmacist; in many of the saner parts of the world, this safe facility will *be* your pharmacist. You can often donate unused and nonrancid cosmetics and other sundries to local homeless shelters. If you really think you might need something, but you haven't needed it in the last year, put it in a box or a bag with a label reading, "Dispose of this after [the date six months from now]."

For bonus points: Now that there's less clutter, take a moment to wipe down all the shelves. *Mmm* ... happy bathroom!

Cast out the snakes

Here's one the techies among us are encouraged to revisit every St. Patrick's Day (or whenever you think of it): Cast out the snakes. You hereby have permission to put all those old audio and video cables, which you've accumulated over the years and are hanging onto "just in case," in your charity box and get them off your island. While you're at it, throw in all the devices you no longer use and chargers for devices you no longer own.

That trick works on the computer, too. Take a few minutes today to look around on your hard drive and find those things you never use and don't want taking up your active space.

Here are some examples of things that you can often delete or back up for your archives:

- All the not-so-good pictures from that digital photo session;

- Programs you never use;

- Really old backups for which all the data have since been added to multiple subsequent backups, or changed so much as to render this version no longer useful;

- Saved chats with that guy or gal with whom things never worked out; and

- 90% of most people's Downloads folder.

Follow the appropriate instructions for uninstalling programs on your computer—and do be careful about system files. If you don't know what they do, get help before deleting them.

Do you really need that car?

This tip is most relevant to city dwellers, but those in the country should also mull over how much vehicle they really need—and how many. Leaving aside the fact that the industrialized world has been hitting snooze on the climate alarm for 30+ years, overemphasizing cars in our lives has a significant impact.

How much do you spend on car payments, repairs, insurance, parking, and tickets? Every time I look at that number for the places I've lived, my average is about $500 a month. I thought about the hassle of driving, parking and protecting a car in the city and I opted out. I could rent a car every weekend and still come out ahead, but whatI found is that I don't really need one very often. I have a membership with our local car sharing service and use it between zero and three times a month. I take a cab an average of two or three times a week. Otherwise, I walk, take public transit, and carpooled when I still had a commute. I save money, get exercise, avoid stress, and dramatically reduce the impact I have on the environment.

What would your life be like if you lived in a vibrant neighborhood where you could walk to shops, restaurants and entertainment? What if your commute gave you time to read, catch up on email, or just stretch your legs? For all that talk about cars helping us stay connected and giving us flexibility, I've found quite the opposite to be true. I'm freer and less isolated the less time I've spent in my personal metal box on wheels.

Discardian Erik Bates eased into things by choosing to experiment with not driving for one month—then two—before deciding about getting rid of his car. Circumstances forced a bolder approach for Discardian Helga Murray. She didn't replace her car when it broke down, and found that switching to public transit turned out great. She enjoys local sightseeing and exercise, saves money, and has less stress, more endurance, and more energy. She rounds out her walking and public transit ridership with infrequent use of taxis and her car sharing membership, plus once a year or so renting a car to go out of town.

Helga says, "I love not having a car. Still don't have one five years later, not planning on getting one, unless for some reason I move out of this area and have to go somewhere without public transportation. Since a city with good public transportation is a minimum requirement for me, I don't see that happening any time soon."

Even if a car is a requirement for you right now, keep an eye on how you use it and see if you could drive it less or share rides more.

Why be where what you want or need to be doing isn't?

When we're thinking about relying less on cars, we are reminded that it's time to start an even bigger "letting go" in much of the western world. We rich nations have got to say farewell to the strange notion that has gripped us for the last half century: our suburban life style—with its two-car garage, McMansions, lawns in the desert, strip malls, and daily auto errands—is unsustainable. There's never going to be more oil or natural gas readily available than there is now. Suburbia relies on these energy sources for its residents to be able to get to shops or work and to heat or cool their very large homes as well as to build the homes and the accoutrements associated with this lifestyle.

More than that, though, is it really such a great lifestyle? Do people form tighter bonds with their neighbors in a residential development park than they do in a mixed-use city block or the countryside? Do people in places with no shops or workplaces within walking distance feel connected to the communities surrounding their neighborhood? If you have to drive to get to anything, how can you overcome feelings of distance from places through which you move?

Talk to those who've moved to the city, away from the disconnected life and void of architectural interest in the 'burbs. For example, Discardians Heather Wright, Chelee Ellis, and Amelia Parker, will tell you about their happiness and the nearby features that show how they're using all that time out of the car.

Heather: "We live five minutes north of downtown, can walk to an organic market, [coffee shop, award-winning local restaurants, bakery], library, pharmacy, etc. We know our neighbors and a healthy number of people in our neighborhood."

Chelee: "We live in town within walking distance of my favorite 4: the library, the grocery store, the park, and a bus stop."

Amelia: "The smaller house (a 1912 bungalow) is three blocks from three grocery stores, one of the local arthouse cinemas, a yoga studio, our vet's office and the biggest urban green space in the city."

Think about what you really love and your minimum requirements, and open yourself to urban possibilities, or at least work to bring some of the good features of cities and smaller residences to your nonurban home.

Of her new neighborhood, Heather Wright also said, "Our two criteria when we were looking for a house: on Saturdays you could hear saws and hammers as people worked on their houses and you also saw parents walking children in strollers. We figured if parents felt safe enough strolling with their kids, it was safe enough for us."

When the life of the neighborhood extends to the street, a place feels more alive. It is amazing to find that it is actually cheaper to rent in the city than own in the suburbs—18% cheaper, according to one article cited by Cynthia Friedlob of *The Thoughtful Consumer*.

Letting go of our back pages

Let us return to a category of things that is very difficult for many people to keep pared down to only what they currently love or use: books. College and earlier textbooks are a common culprit. If it's been over five years since you have used that book, let it go. Should you ever need that information again, you'll find a more current and easily searchable version online. Got some books that you don't know why you have? Donate them. If you're worried that you might someday need to remember their titles—"What was the name of that book I read?"—take pictures of their covers, save the picture in your digital photo album, and tag it "Books I've read." Then, get rid of the physical, space-taking, dust-gathering objects.

Send books on to a new life elsewhere when they stop having a positive interaction in yours. Slow the flow of incoming books by being more selective when you choose to buy a book rather than borrow it from the library. Note that not all good reasons for *buying* are also good reasons for *keeping*. Letting go now doesn't remove the book from the universe. "Maybe I'll want to reread it someday" is a weak reason to hold on to this particular copy in a world with libraries, used bookstores, Amazon, OpenLibrary, Google Book Search, and trading websites like Swap.com.

Books are more available now than at any other time in history. Thanks to the Internet, we now have access to the inventories of more new and used bookstores and libraries than any one person could browse in a lifetime, as well as to the collections of individuals who are willing to share or trade. Beyond that, we have more new and old books available in electronic form.

As society goes through this transition to digital abundance, many people have kept up internal expectations of how much on-paper reading we're going to do, even as our on-screen reading—and writing!—have grown tremendously. A good Discardian act is to give ourselves credit for the many ways we're connecting to ideas and to others and start calibrating our expectations more appropriately.

Pop-culture writer Linda Holmes faced this chasm between our expectations of ourselves and reality in her *National Public Radio* post, "The Sad, Beautiful Fact That We're All Going to Miss Almost Everything," saying, "Well-read is not a destination; there is nowhere to get to, and if you assume there is somewhere to get to, you'd have to live a thousand years to even think about getting there, and by the time you got there, there would be a thousand years to catch up on."

Instead of running a futile race to keep up with the amazing explosion of human creative output, explore thoughtfully and with conscious delight the abundance from which you can choose.

While you're easing your expectations of the amount of deeply focused reading you're going to do, give yourself credit for the positive aspects of all the other ways you're connecting with ideas. As science author Steven Johnson has pointed out, "Quiet contemplation has led to its fair share of important thoughts. But it cannot be denied that good ideas also emerge in networks. ... The speed with which we can follow the trail of an idea, or discover new perspectives on a problem, has increased by several orders of magnitude. We are marginally less focused, and exponentially more connected. That's a bargain all of us should be happy to make."

So, if you can get pretty much any book you want again later, what guidelines will you use for why you should keep a book in your house?

Here are mine:

- I'm going to read or reread it within four years. (This will drop to two years once I catch up with the wave of books I recently swapped for and am ignoring as I spend more time writing than reading.)

- I consult it at least once a year.

- I periodically reread or consult it, and which contains annotations that remain useful to me.

- It is an object of beauty or sentiment, which brings me frequent joy.

- I wrote it.

Decide your guidelines and then look to see what you have that doesn't meet any of them. Donate those replaceable (or never again needed) books to the library or charity. Give the stuff you love more room and give yourself less unnecessary weight of stuff in your life.

Someday is now

What do you have that you were saving for later?

It's later.

Do you want it?

If not, *get rid of it*.

You probably won't need that exact thing again. In the rare times that you do, the hassle of re-acquiring it is much less trouble than the hassle of working around 90+% of the stuff you never would have needed again anyway. Living lighter makes you much more flexible for dealing with very occasional exceptions.

What about feeling stressed over letting *this* thing go? If you're finding it extremely hard to part with something that you don't use or find beautiful, you may need to give it a time out. Seal those things up in a box and write on the top, side, and end (so you can read it in a stack of boxes), "Re-evaluate on [the date six months from today]."

Don't write what's in the box. Put a reminder in your calendar to look through it. When you open it, you may find it useful to discover things you'd totally erased from your mind. Maybe they just needed time off from use; often, though, you'll find that now you're really ready to send them on to a new home. This can be a great exercise to do with kids. Either the toy is now forgotten and boring or it's almost like a new toy. Either way is a win!

When you hang onto something with a particular future intention, make sure to attach a "Do By" date label. For example, I had a bunch of goofy old things that I thought would be fun surprise presents for a Pirate Gift Exchange (in which participants on their turn either open a wrapped present or steal from another player). I held onto that box of random weirdness for *years* without ever throwing that party, and finally wound up giving the stuff to charity. I should have donated it much earlier or been forced by a scheduled deadline into having the party. Replace that nebulous "someday" with a specific plan for the not-too-distant future ... or decide now.

Clutter Everywhere

19

You Need What You Need, but You Don't Need Much More Than You Need

> How terrible would it be if you needed
> a glass jar and didn't have one?
> — *Gretchen Rubin, author*

So much stuff

If you combine mass production and rising standards of living over the past century, pretty much anyone outside the Third World can have more belongings than they'll ever need—and more than their homes can accommodate. This reality reached a fever pitch after the 1960s as real disposable personal income per capita in the United States grew and spending increased while prices for most goods dropped dramatically. By the 1990s, heftily squatting on the scales opposite voluntary simplicity and similar movements, the average American family had twice as many possessions as their counterpart 25 years prior, according to a September 2009 article by Jon Mooallem in *The New York Times*, "The Self-Storage Self—Storing All the Stuff We Accumulate."

You don't need to turn to the most extreme cases—illustrated in lurid detail in the TV series *Hoarders*, for instance—to see that we all have examples of this cultural dysfunction impacting our lives. So much stuff. So constant a habit of acquisition with little or no corresponding habit of shedding the excess. Little wonder that focusing your attention on things with which you've surrounded yourself can feel like emerging from a long-term drug or alcohol haze. We wake from our collective bender and groan at the weight of our gluttony.

This may not seem like that big a deal—why not keep that box of clothes you wore in college or your thrashed childhood skateboard?—but it's an enormous problem. Writer and thoughtful consumer Cynthia Friedlob cut to the heart of it: "Clutter doesn't just crowd your home, it crowds your life. It prevents you from living fully in the moment, from feeling comfortable in your surroundings, from using your time to do the meaningful things that would bring you happiness."

More than just a personal issue that everyone needs to examine in their own lives, it's also a cultural issue on a massive scale. Mooallem also noted that the United States now has 2.3 billion square feet of self-storage space—more than seven square feet for every man, woman, and child in the country—despite the size of the average American home almost doubling in the past 50 years.

Non-Americans: Don't look smug. As Boris Johnson pointed out in 2009, Europe has started to follow the same path: "If the self-storage industry keeps growing at this rate, the day is not far off when we will all be Tutankhamuns, trying to cheat death with a secret funerary display of all the things that are most personally suggestive, most symbolic of our lives, and the things we couldn't bear to chuck."

Ten percent of households in the U.S. have a self-storage unit, according to the Self Storage Association, a nonprofit trade group, and as cited by Mooallem. That means that one in 10 households pays money every month to put things they that don't want in their homes into a place where they can delay deciding what to do about them.

Read that again: Lots of people pay extra to keep things they're pretty sure they don't need.

Decide! *In or out!* It won't kill you and it just might turn your life around. At any rate, it will give you money that you can apply toward your real and current goals and dreams instead of frittering it away as a tithe to the Church of Procrastination.

Deciding shouldn't be as hard as it seems to be. Fifteen percent of self-storage customers described themselves as using their units to store items they "no longer need or want." Even knowing this, they found it to be a better decision to pay money every month not to have to make choices about that stuff. Dishearteningly, Mooallem reported that storing the unwanted "was the third-most-popular use for a unit and was projected to grow to 25 percent of renters the following year."

Can you picture me with my mouth open, blinking at the article as I read that? *Are we crazy?* Maybe not crazy but in profound denial. TV critic and author Heather Havrilesky said, "We all want to feel that our lives are filled with endless possibilities, that we have all the time in the world. Hoarding can be a way of denying that there's an end point to your timeline or boundaries around your opportunities."

Limits don't prevent fulfillment; they're merely the edges of the canvas. Make your life a masterpiece in the space and time you have.

I can see viewing a storage unit as a temporary workspace for the project of weeding through a backlog of possessions while gaining the immediate benefit of a less-crowded home, but I am dubious about taking on both the cost and the risk of depending on that extra slack to hoard things that aren't of real value to you.

One member of the online community MetaFilter bearing the enigmatic handle "Pastabagel," summarized the danger like this: "Don't just accumulate stuff in a warehouse. You'll turn your junk into a utility bill."

Uncover your comfort level

Clutter is both the low-hanging fruit and the pernicious beast in the process of freeing your life of stuff that you don't actually want in it. Discardia has made me—who has never been a neatnik—able to have my house ready for company with a couple minutes of tidying up. It turns out living with clutter is far more work than maintaining a cleaner place. Your comfort level may be more or less messy than mine. I'm tidier than mess-loving folks, but less so than some I know with pristine homes and perfectly ordered closets.

Regardless of where you position yourself on the spectrum, it matters that your home isn't full of things you don't want, blocking your enjoyment of what you do. Think of the cottage-style garden with flowers spilling out in clumps. Embrace your particular mess and ruthlessly prune away any junk that detracts from your happiness.

It's uncanny how much our feelings of personal freedom are connected to the amount of wiggle room our stuff has. Ask yourself, "What could I remove that would make this space (or time) work better?" We radically improved the intimacy and spaciousness of our living room by rearranging everything and, most importantly, by removing three pieces of furniture. It's now more supportive of really living in it, doing what we most value: conversation and relaxed contemplation.

———

Here are a few more little laps to keep cutting away what you don't need:

Why do you have more than one of those? You only need one of certain things, so why clutter up your life with multiples? Are you actually the kind of person who ever uses a multihead screwdriver in each hand? While I understand the existence of an extra can opener in the emergency kit, do you really need three in the kitchen drawer? There's a store (or a relative's overstocked drawer) nearby where you can get another if this one breaks. Keep the best one and get rid of the inferiors. For some things—corkscrews, for example—it's worth having one spare so a broken tool doesn't ruin an evening. (However, if there's a corkscrew on your Swiss army knife—as there is on mine—you've got your emergency backup, so get rid of the big extras.)

Some tools and steps aren't required at all. Examine the order in which you do things. Are you needlessly creating a wasteful requirement? For example, if you simply put the cream and sugar in your coffee cup before you pour in the coffee, would you need that little wooden or plastic coffee stirrer? Tune in to how other people perform tasks and see if their methods are simpler. While you're thinking about tools, keep an eye out for those that no longer apply to how you live. If your household is now vegetarian, maybe that turkey roasting rack and extra sets of steak knives can go, eh?

When was the last time you used a printed phone book? ... and the time before that? I can't even remember when it was. I look everything up online now. If that's you, too, then contact your phone company or visit the National Yellow Pages Consumer Choice & Opt-Out Site and opt out of receiving them. If you do use the printed books, though, keep the latest and only copy. Search around your house and purge those old phone books to the recycling bin. Multi-inch thick, instantly out-of-date giant bricks of paper take up a bunch of space for very little value these days.

Have fewer and better. Go through your dishes and pans. Donate any that would never be your first choice. Identify anything that you need to replace or upgrade. This could mean buying a better-made brand—my heavy-duty, nonstick cookware has definitely improved my quality of life—but it could also mean keeping an eye out in thrift stores for wonderful vintage replacements for dull modern goods. (My cocktail parties have eclectic glasses, which cheerfully reflect the diverse characters holding them.) When finding what you'll love and use, the question "Will I kick myself for a year if I don't get this charming thing?" is as valid as "Would I remember in a few years that I once got this?" Don't save the "best" dishes for some magic day. Find a way for them to make you happy every week.

Coming in, going out

As ever, it's about seeing and deciding. Ask yourself, "Why do I have this? If I lost it, would or could I replace it?" Not everything you wouldn't replace needs to be discarded, but a negative answer can be an indicator of something unimportant of which you'll be letting go before too long or of something important of which you may want to document the memory.

When bringing new things into your home, ask, "Does this replace or render unneeded something else?" Whether as a short-term exercise to help you understand your habits or a strict zero-sum approach to life, try having a place in mind for anything you want to buy. If there's already something there, either it goes or decide not to buy the new thing.

When reviewing what you already have in your home, ask, "Have I used this in the last two years?" If not, let it go. One British Discardian, with the fine nom de web "Ruut Ackses," has used this method to own nothing but the essentials, which are regularly used, plus some nice art. That technique in combination with the philosophy "stuff is just stuff … not your friends or your family," has created a comfortable life with a lightened load.

While you progress through your uncluttering projects, keep an eye out for things you have lost or forgotten, which could serve a vibrant role in your life. As professional organizer Jeri Dansky says, it's a treasure hunt. Whether the treasure you find turns out to be an object that takes a new active role, some lost travelers' checks, or a gloriously empty shelf in the closet, there's gold to be found! (The stuff that isn't treasure to you could be to someone else; let it go to where it is needed.)

The beautiful essentials

Find your own rewards in having only the right things for you. When editor and author Diana Athill chose to move into a retirement home at the age of 92, she said she knew that it was the sensible thing to do, and was happily surprised to find it lucky as well. She wrote of the change, "At breakfast today I sat in my little room thinking how odd it is that I never get bored by my things. Then I realised that nothing in the room is here out of habit, or because it was given me by dear old so-and-so, or because I couldn't be bothered to get rid of it. Everything, from the carpet to the biscuit tin and including of course the too-many pictures, ornaments and books, is here because, however uninteresting it might be to others, I love it. It's as though 'possessing' has been distilled down from being a vague pleasure to being an intense one: less is more."

Columnist Mark Morford put it very succinctly: "Clear out your clutter. Strip it all to the beautiful essentials and then keep it that way."

20

Too Many Clothes

Closet Tricks

> There are three great design themes: making
> something beautiful, making something easier,
> and making something possible.
> —*Dan Saffer, interaction designer and author*

There is a better way

Many people live for years with overstuffed closets where finding the right thing to wear is hard. Pulling one piece out knocks others off their hangers. Clothes don't look their best because they've been jammed tightly together. Why make yourself crazy with something so basic as getting dressed?

The reverse clothes hanger trick

Close your eyes and imagine the benefits you could be enjoying as you trade quality for quantity with your clothing. You'd have space in closets and drawers, no bad choices to work around, a release from emotional baggage, the ability to see what pieces you still need to create your ideal wardrobe, plus the opportunity to recombine clothes in fresh ways and to rethink your identity. Sounds good, yes? So how to knock out that fabric logjam?

Start thinking of your closet as a service rather than a collection and make a habit of staying on the right service plan with only the features you need. Here's a tip I've heard many times, from organizer Peter Walsh and others, and have used with great success on my own closets: Twice a year, turn around all the hangers so the hooks are pointing toward you. When you wear something, put it back with the hook the normal way. Put a reminder in your calendar for six months later to get rid of the things that are still wrong-way-round. The shoe equivalent of turning around your hangers is to put a penny in the toe. In six months, give away the shoes that still have their pennies.

Throughout the year, as you handle all your clothes keep an eye out for anything that is so worn or stained that you wouldn't want to be seen in it and toss it. Take anything that is two sizes or more too small or too large and put it in your charity box. If something fills you with negative emotions as soon as you see it, get it out of your life.

Whenever you put something on and it doesn't quite fit, but you look at it and like it enough that you'd buy it again now if it did fit, put it at the back of your closet to revisit in six months. I put the top of the hanger through a square of colored paper to easily spot these "Don't bother trying me on right now" things and avoid them when getting dressed. If they still don't fit in six months, pick a few favorites and shop for replacement versions in your size. Repeat the process until you've let go of everything that isn't great for you now.

Build your discarding muscles

Writer and cartoonist Chris Onstad, through the voice of his character Cornelius Bear, wisely selected the closet as an ideal place to build the habit of cutting the crap from your life: "Go into your closet, find a shirt you haven't worn in fifteen years ... and drop it straight into the kitchen trash. There. How did that feel? A little snag of remorse as it hit bottom? That feeling is your salvation. Come to know it, and embrace it, and recognize that it, like a burning muscle the day after a good run, is actually the feeling of healing."

Seasonal culls

The change of the seasons into summer and winter is a good time to revisit things in your closet. It gives you a chance to look again at clothes you haven't worn since last year and decide if you love them enough to renew their contract as players on your team. When the chill grows in the air, go through all those coats, sweaters, scarves, mittens, and boots, and decide what you're going to wear within the next 30 days. If it doesn't make the cut, get rid of it. Someone else needs to be warm more than you need to maintain "The Gallery of Unwanted Winterwear." As the sunshine blooms and you shed layers, do the same thing with bathing suits, shorts, lightweight dresses, halter tops, sandals, and t-shirts.

Cartoon by Jimmy Johnson, Arlo & Janis.
Used by permission of the author.

Don't hang onto things that you never use. Send that just-not-you suit to one of the great organizations helping low-income businesspeople carry themselves to success. Give that big, out-of-fashion winter coat to charity and save someone from the chill. Let that over-the-top formal-wear send someone on a tight budget to the prom or a holiday party in style. Move the neglected items out of your space and into the arms of someone who really appreciates them.

Remember: "Someday Is Now" still applies to your dress clothes; we simply define "Now" as being a longer time range. When you haven't worn that suit or gown in six months, but you don't want to be in the lurch if you get invited to a fancy occasion, you can still hold onto it "just in case," provided that it fits you well and you actually like wearing it. However, I have seen people keep something ostensibly because they think, "I might need to wear it if I go to a formal event," but really for the reason "I spent too much on this and it fits me completely wrong and I haven't worn it the last five times I've been invited to a formal event, but maybe, if I hold onto it, *somehow* that money will magically have been wisely spent."

Keep things that are both beautiful and useful to you, and perhaps define the utility of formals in a longer-than-six-month cycle, but move the rest along. Don't let the fear of being caught unprepared for exceptional events make your daily encounter with your closet a hassle.

The best possible

My friend, entrepreneur Evan Williams, gave me a wonderful tip for choosing whether to keep or buy clothes: "Don't ask, 'Can I imagine wearing this?' Instead, ask 'Can I imagine this ever being the best possible thing in my closet to wear?'" (This approach works extremely well for other things besides clothes!)

Listen to your answers about what is "the best possible thing to wear." You will find that it represents a smaller list of clothes than most people own—and certainly less than the fashion industry would like you to buy.

> Dress for your own happiness, convenience, and the message you want to send to the world.

You may find that all you really need is a core set of underlying pieces, which you mix and match to suit activities, mood, and weather. If you have doubts about how far you can go with a single, simple base garment, look no further than the amazing array of styles achieved in Sheena Matheiken's first year of *The Uniform Project*. How about other experiments like the *Six Items or Less Challenge*, Courtney Carver's *Project 333*, or the constant color adventure the "wear nothing new" outfits designer Jessi Arrington shares on her blog *Lucky So and So?* Great quality over quantity tips are also available in Jesse Thorn and Adam Lisagor's web series *Put This On*.

Extreme immediate change isn't necessary—this is Discardia, after all, and there's no need to be mean to yourself—so take a step in the direction of reducing unrewarding shopping, owning fewer clothes that make you look and feel less than great, and spending less time worrying over what to wear.

When nothing in your closet is wrong for you, getting dressed can cease to be a source of stress and hassle.

21

Stuff as a Way to Show You Care

The Lamp Has No Feelings

> What global psychological hang-up prevents people
> from throwing away dried-up erasable markers, the
> moment they notice them?
> —*David Allen*

Not antistuff, just pro-awesome

We hold onto things out of a need for security; however, other more subtle, sometimes toxic, emotional responses are behind packrat tendencies. Look in any room of your house and you can probably find past gifts, likely as not a bit dusty but rarely discarded.

Physical manifestations of past moments of connectedness are a good thing, yes. You should surround yourself with what makes you remember that you are liked and loved. However, look harder and see how many things you keep out of a sense of duty to that ideal and for no other reason—things that are neither beautiful nor useful, take up space, need to be moved and cleaned, and slowly become emotionally dull, and yet are not cast off.

How many things in your house purely represent your affection for someone but which, as objects, you would otherwise not choose to have? That slightly tacky jewelry from your deceased great-aunt that you never wear but which you wouldn't want to hurt her posthumous feelings by donating to charity? The vaguely comical refrigerator magnet you received as a farewell present from your favorite coworker at your job before last, which he's never seen again since he's never been to your house and you haven't been in touch for months anyhow?

We fear that by rejecting the thing, we reject the person. We worry that parting with the physical reminder will erase the memory and the emotion.

Hesitating to part with unwanted things out of an impulse to be kind makes even less sense when we relate to our belongings as though they could be emotionally wounded by our behavior. It doesn't matter to a chair whether you've had it for 10 days or 10 years. It won't care if you give it away. If you've stopped caring about it, there's no reason not to act on that change. Who are you worried about offending? In the words of the wonderful Ikea ad by Spike Jonze, "Many of you feel bad for this lamp. That is because you're crazy. It has no feelings—and the new one is much better."

Let it go.

There are ways to remember other than bearing all these objects around with us like Marley's chains. It's fine—even commendable—to part with this physical stuff. Even good stuff can move on to make room for the life you're living now or want to be living in the future.

Even the sweetest stuff can find a new home

Don't assume that there is a direct correlation between unwillingness to let something go and the intensity of the memories it evokes. When I was helping my parents move out of the house in which I'd grown up, I opened a door into an attic room, saw the object in front of me, and was hit full force by a vivid, emotional memory.

I'm four. My mother is holding me in her arms rocking me slowly in a white, wooden rocking chair. She is singing a lullaby. I am hearing the lullaby and feeling the safeness of her loving arms. I am feeling the gentle sway of the movement of the chair lulling me down comfortably.

I am standing, leaning forward with the attic door latch in my right hand, looking at the white rocking chair a few feet in front of me. That object had some mighty strong mojo, no doubt about it. I don't remember now if I cried; I suspect that I did as I rocked in that lovely, sturdy, old chair. Of all the things in that house, you would think that the chair would be most likely to be sitting in my home now, but it's not. That chair needs to rock babies to sleep. That chair needs to hold little children with their fingers in their mouths listening to fairy tales.

I'd already decided years ago not to have kids, which was perhaps the most significant Discardian choice of my life for its impact on my carbon footprint as well as the space it's created for other opportunities. Because of this decision, I knew the chair needed to be with someone else. I gave it to friends, who were pregnant with their first child, so that it could serve at least one more generation and create happy childhood memories. Perhaps if I'd taken the chair my memories would have become diluted. Maybe sometimes the most emotionally significant things need to be preserved in our hearts rather than in our homes.

———

Send even the sentimental stuff on to a new home when the time comes. This "Free if you come and get it" offer appeared on my old company's community email list, which illustrates beautifully that even the most special item sometimes reaches the end of its life with you: "Fifteen years ago, my wife came home with this giant earth-mover tire on top of our Toyota. It's about three feet across (maybe a little more), and weighs a whole lot. We stood it up next to our kids' play structure, buried it about one-quarter of the way into the dirt, and it provided years of climbing and sliding fun. Now, the kids are teenagers, and seem to have lost interest in it. Fickle!"

You do not need to maintain a physical museum of everything you or your kids touch. Take photos of those Lego creations then break the pieces apart and tell new stories. Scan or photograph that artwork and use it for your computer screensaver or desktop. You can print it out again in a pinch. Convert atoms to bits where possible and give yourself permission to forget. Participation rather than preservation is often the better goal.

What about presents?

So someone gave you something and either you didn't want to keep it from the start or you've outgrown it in one sense or another. Tell me: When you visit the homes of your friends and family, do you check to see if your past gifts are in use? If they aren't, are you more likely to be hurt and upset with them than think, "Hmm, whoops, guess that wasn't really the right thing; I'll try a gift certificate next time"? If the answer to both questions is "yes," consider yourself spanked and cut it out. It isn't doing you or anyone else any good.

How can you part with unwanted gifts without considering it an insult to the giver? Give everyone permission not to be able to read your mind and give yourself (and others) permission to change. The intent of gift giving is to make someone feel good or to repay a social obligation. Recognize the act and the intent. Perhaps keep the gift around for a courteous amount of time, but on no account lie excessively about how much you like things you don't like because you'll set yourself up for a matching bad gift the next time.

Once you have observed the necessary niceties enough to communicate your gratitude for the intent, part with unwanted gifts without guilt. Disposing of them may require more discretion than with other things—the yard sale that the giver is likely to attend is a bad method, but the bottom of your Goodwill bag covered by that shirt that doesn't fit anymore is just dandy. Quietly get rid of it and if the giver asks about it later, say something about your appreciation of the occasion and their thoughtfulness. If you're worried that they're going to give you another equally undesired gift, you may want to confess that it didn't go with your other things.

Note: A great deal of hard work was put into some gifts. For these, it is most honest to come clean and let the giver have the opportunity to take back their artistic efforts rather than sneakily disposing of it. Bite the bullet and say, "I really appreciate your making me something so special. I am impressed by your thoughtfulness. Unfortunately, this painting just doesn't fit with the rest of my decor/I don't wear the color of this hand-knit sweater/I'm allergic to taxidermied animals ... " Whatever. It might be a rough conversation, but it's better hearing them say, "You gave away my masterpiece to Goodwill?" or "You *lied* to me about having kept it!"

How do you get better gifts? Tell people what you want, especially if what you want is nothing. Also, for those whose perception of your tastes is consistently dead wrong (or for everyone if you're planning a cross-country move), let them know that you really want an experience, like dinner or some movie tickets, or, even safer, a donation to one of your favorite charities.

Needless Obligation

Remember What's Optional

22

> The truly free person is one who can turn down an
> invitation to dinner without giving an excuse. Learn to
> say no simply: "Sorry. I won't be able to join you." Period.
> —*Elaine St. James, author and simplicity guru*

Overexpectant

Don't let imaginary obligations stress you out when it comes to things other than gifts. Remember that you have the option to move on or opt out when it becomes nonideal. Why slog on to "wildly frustrated"?

Sometimes we act as though we have a lot more loaded on ourselves than we really do. We set up these expectations—not even with others, necessarily, but with ourselves—that can then prevent us from meeting real deadlines without feeling overwhelmed.

Yes, it's good to set goals and keep up with them. Yes, it leads to improved skills or other benefits. However, ya don't gotta do it all! Think about how required your "must do" things really are. Overcommitted? Check your to-do's for any items better described as "Someone else can do it better," "Someone else can do it just fine," and "It no longer needs to be done."

Discardian and creative and cultural industry consultant Helga Henry described her process of doing this: "I got rid of some mental clutter. There were a couple of projects I wasn't getting on with. Week after week, incomplete tasks from this project got transferred from one to-do list to the next. My heart sank each time I thought about them.

Why were they dragging me down—why couldn't I muster up the energy to do quite simple tasks like make a call or write an email about them?

"Well, when I took time to think about it—it was because they were not really MY projects. They were initiatives that I felt that I 'ought' to do, or that I took on because I wanted to feel or be useful. I had no real passion (an overused word, but I mean it in this context) or desire to achieve the goals of these projects. On one project because, actually, I think the moment had passed and what was originally a good idea had been overtaken by events and on the other because I was in a group that seemed to be a bit indecisive and I wanted to make something happen so just agreed to a heap of actions because I was annoyed.

"Once I had seen this—I took steps to give those projects back. I didn't just abandon them, but I made it clear what actions I was going to take to hand over responsibility and then I handed them over. I immediately felt better."

Graciously decline to overload yourself

Things that you have to do by a certain time or on a certain day will sometimes add up to a large list. This is the time to make an agreement with yourself to put other things on hold. If a low-stress window comes along while those things are set aside and you feel like doing one of them, that's great, but do not feel a speck of guilt over making a plan to opt out of optional activities for a set period of time. If you're worried about losing track of these desires and ideas put them on your someday-maybe list and look at them again later. Keep yourself happy and relaxed and rewarded now.

A big part of remembering what's optional is the art of saying "no." Being clear with yourself about your priorities and realistic about your available time allows you to make smart decisions about whether something can fit into your world right now or not.

Quality over quantity is a great principle to follow in food and drink, as well as in how much you try to fit into your calendar or the goals on which you're actively working. Remember the difference between "have to" and "want to." Stressing out should never be on your have-to list.

My mother lives in a remote area and is a member of a book group in her old college town many hours away. In a letter, along with news of car repairs for one of the family vehicles, she described this moment of internal debate: "On the drive home from the mechanic, I suddenly realized that it made every kind of sense to skip the book group this time. The van is not comfortable for me to drive for long distances, and also if I took it, Paul would be without transportation for two days. And I really felt like going to sleep fairly early, not staying up late to finish the book. By the time I got home I was convinced, and I've continued to feel very good about that decision—in fact every little while a wave of elation sweeps over me, with the realization that I'll have two days mostly at home instead of two days of hurrying on the road."

When letting go is an incredibly invigorating choice, don't be silly—let go!

Not everything started must be finished

If it's not rewarding or otherwise serving your goals, stop doing it. Get rid of that unenjoyable, third-of-the-way-through book. Remove those things that no longer interest you from your someday-maybe list. As writer and designer D. Keith Robinson put it, "In order to do something great not only do you need a good idea to start with, you need to be able to focus on that idea and execute. It's hard to focus when you have so many things going on. Sometimes you've got to let things go."

Know when to quit and put your positive energy instead into something that will help you to become who you want to be.

Do the math

Don't assume that you are always obligated to achieve the best possible outcome—and certainly don't assume that you could even if you tried. One of the benefits of growing older and having experienced more things is that you get better at estimating how things will work out. This skill is worth improving and utilizing whenever you're deciding if something is worth doing.

Here's an example: Let's say you have a bunch of stuff you want to discard. You do, yes? Yes. It can be tough to make the call between "sell" and "give away." We often lean toward sell because we feel guilty about just giving away something on which we spent money or which was a gift; however, it's not always the best path. Look over what you have and roughly decide its price and how long it would take you to handle all aspects of selling it. Now look at what you'd get paid per hour for that time and decide if it's an hourly wage worth trying to earn.

There's a tradeoff between time spent and money gained. One way to offset that is to add something to the gain side of the equation by trying to have its new location make you happy. In my experience, unless I'm really scraping by financially, selling stuff is more work than it's worth. If you have a broke friend who's interested, you might take those charity boxes and say, "Hey, do you want to try to sell this? You can have 75% of what you make off of it." Otherwise, donate it and take the tax deduction or throw the dang stuff away and figure that you've earned a beautiful, less-cluttered new home.

———

Sometimes, maybe often, the best choice is to cut your losses and get the nonmonetary benefit of clearing out of your way those distractions that keep you from the life you want to be living.

23

Life Out of Balance

Don't Live in Overdrive

> Do not believe that it is very much of an advance to
> do the unnecessary three times as fast.
> —*Peter Drucker, writer and management consultant*

Build your day

Author and coach Nigel Marsh was right when he said, "The reality of the society that we're in is there are thousands and thousands of people out there leading lives of quiet, screaming desperation where they work long, hard hours at jobs they hate, to enable them to buy things they don't need, to impress people they don't like."

Hamsters running on their wheels should not be our role models. Spinning faster and getting nowhere isn't achievement. Instead of burning yourself out working too hard on things that don't help you reach your goals, improve your habits, or understand your dreams, cool down and apply your time and energy strategically.

> Start off your day by building it out of the right pieces. First, think of the way you'd spend the day if you had no obligations at all, if you could do whatever you want. Second, identify those things that must happen today or else tomorrow will suck. Third, note the commitments you made to other people and social possibilities you'd already been considering that still sound appealing. Now, build a day that has all three represented, with adequate time between so you don't feel rushed. I recommend cutting from piece three to ensure you get enough of piece one. You can't do everything, so do what you love most, what helps you avoid hassles, and what keeps you connected with those who matter to you. Of course it's hard to have those perfect days, especially when you're first starting out, but know what they look like so you can steer the days you do have toward them.

Prime your pump

When your energy is low or you're recovering from a big disruption in your normal routine, try the advice of writer and minimalist Erin Doland: "Schedule the task you will feel the greatest reward from accomplishing first. You need momentum to propel you through the next task, which will be the thing you need to do the most." You may not be able to get back to normal today, but getting at least these two things done will help you on that path.

If you're feeling disconnected, think of someone you know who really energizes you or helps you sort out where you want to be heading and schedule lunch or dinner with one of those people within the next two weeks. Not only will you do better work in the afternoons if you aren't always eating at your desk, staying in touch with friends and mentors gives a feeling of having done something for yourself—even on days when you work late or don't have energy in the evening. You have to eat anyway, so turn that into quality time.

Recharge your energy

Even when work is at its crazymaking worst, you do have options and some control. If the workday is a steady race against an enormous set of goals, clocking out should be filled with free time, flexibility, open-ended playing, easily conquered projects chosen to match your mood and energy, and the option to do nothing in particular at all. It's really truly definitely okay that you can't Do It All all the time. In order to give your best when you *are* giving, give your batteries time to recharge—even when that means backing off on social activities or projects.

The quick picture

Facing a busy week ahead? Take five minutes to give yourself the big picture that will help you manage your time. Grab a sheet of scratch paper, make five equal sections to represent the next five days, and then sketch into them roughly proportional squares for the events and chunks of work that must fit into those days. This may reveal things you need to cancel or reduce the scope or detail of work to be achievable in the available time. Give yourself a ballpark estimate of what you have lined up for yourself and use it as a tool to adjust unrealistic expectations.

A similar quick-sketch technique for preparing yourself or others—particularly when you need to decide priorities—is the Three-Column Briefing. Again, grab a piece of scratch paper or use a whiteboard, and make three columns. Label them "What?," "Why?," and "How?" In the first column, write the task that needs to be done; in the second, what purpose or goal it serves; in the third, the end state, in other words, how it should look when it's done. If you use this technique to plan work with a team, you can also use the third column to indicate who will do that task. Keep this at a high level and use this tool to align your actions with your vision of where what you want to achieve. When a task doesn't serve your top goals, it will stick out like a sore thumb in the "Why?" column.

Stay calm. Plan your work. Work your plan. Take a breath, see where you stand, remind yourself of where you are going, and proceed in a way that takes better care of you.

Keeping control when things get crazy

"Crazy Ivan" is a trick I keep in my toolbox for the most hectic times. One of my coaching clients from an intense startup environment and I were working on ways in which she could get through a hectic time while her department was critically understaffed. As we brainstormed about how she could make progress on goals while working in such an overloaded and interruption-heavy environment, we hit on the idea of using the handicap of never having an hour—and rarely a half hour—available to focus.

Whenever she could grab a breath and choose her next task, she'd look at the clock. If it was in the top half of the hour, she'd put in the next chunk of time (until she inevitably got pulled away for a short while) working on a task for one of her internal goals; if the time was in the bottom of the hour, she'd work on an external goal involving client contact. In this way, by the end of the day, she would have mentally checked in and made progress on both aspects of her role as a department leader multiple times throughout the day. Why "Crazy Ivan"? Well, it turned out that we were both *Hunt for Red October* fans!

———

Sometimes things slip a bit out of control, which can feel like you've lost all the ground you'd gained, but don't panic! Just get back to basics. Suppose you're at home and sick for the third workday in a row. The pessimist in you is moaning about how you're "wasting" your paid time off and the email is piling up at the office and you'll have to overdo it to get things under any kind of control again and this cold won't go away and blah blah blah.

To still that voice, get yourself back to a level of normality. Re-establish your baseline, starting from the spots where you recharge (e.g., bedroom or comfy chair). Breathe deeply. Take 10 long breaths and let them out slowly. Take a shower and shave, or at least wash your face, hands and the back of your neck. Brush and floss your teeth and splash a little mouthwash around in there. Make sure you're up to date on your medicines and water consumption. Put on some comfortable clothes. Collect the trash and recyclables and put them by the door. Make a cup of tea. Open the curtains and let in some light. Decide on one—just one—thing that you *need* to do and do that thing without being pulled off in other distractions. When that's done, decide one thing you'd really *like* to do (e.g., read a fun book, watch a movie, play a game, call a friend, whatever) and do that. Don't panic. It's all going to come out fine.

———

A bedtime tip: When bad things are happening about which you can do nothing, give yourself something else to think about before settling down to sleep. I find CuteOverload.com can often assist.

Burnout isn't worth it

One last note about extremes: If you're routinely burning yourself out at work and coming home stressed but don't see a way to get your boss to balance the load better, STOP. Stop before it stops you. Chronically bad resource management is often the problem of your employer, not you.

This is not a nice, allegorical idea I invented from idle thoughts. One weekend, my father, whose work had been especially demanding of late, felt tension in his chest that was unlike heartburn. He had radiating pain out to his arm. His dad had died of heart failure; thus my father—wise fellow—went to the emergency room right away. They kept him over the weekend for observation. On Monday, they did an angiogram and found his arteries to be over 85% blocked.

The doctor said, "Tomorrow or the day after, we will give you a quadruple bypass."

On Wednesday he had surgery; on Thursday, after having the front of his body opened up and the arteries into his heart altered, he was recovering very nicely. His life hit the reset button. He decided then that things were going to change and his employer would have to work it out. In fact, they did just that without much trouble at all.

Don't wait for your body to force this decision on you. If a situation is killing you, don't let it get away with murder.

24

Rushing

Cash That Sanity Check

> I've been working on bringing more balance to
> my life. To do this, I've had to learn to unplug and
> recharge. To trade multi-tasking for uni-tasking
> and—occasionally—no-tasking. It's left me
> healthier, happier, and more able to try to make a
> difference in the world. My eyes have been opened
> to the value of regularly closing them.
> —*Arianna Huffington, author and political columnist*

Discardia isn't only about things

You can also build up too much unneeded *intangible* stuff. Make your well-being a priority today. Go for a walk to somewhere you can sit and think for a bit. No need to think big thoughts, unless you feel like it; just let the low-level noise fade away. I recommend the beach, but a hillside, park, or quiet corner at the museum can do the job. Go where you won't hear other people's conversations or see any advertisements. Sit and be still. Do nothing. Pull yourself out of your head and into a quiet space. Then, when you've slowed yourself down and gotten out of your worka-day brain race, take a look at what's taking up your mental space.

Drop the worries for today

Some days we feel as if we've been running nonstop for months. Work is hectic, the social calendar fills up, and it seems like even our to-do-for-fun list gets overwhelming. When you reach that point, you need to recharge. If your family or social obligations are always too pressing on the weekends, take a vacation day. You deserve to feel well and happy.

Clear your day—or at least three or four hours of it—of all activities, except those that will reduce your stress and energize you.

What have you been needing and neglecting? Sleep? Hugs? Healthy food? Creative play? Physical activity? Make time for that. Go outside and look for signs of the changing seasons. Take a nap. Listen to old favorite songs. Do something you really love doing without worrying about what anyone else thinks. Head to the movies. Make things out of Legos. Dance. Take a stack of paper or your journal or a computer with the Internet connection turned off, and start writing wishes, stories, grievances, plans, poetry, prose, porn, or pie charts—it doesn't matter. Let out whatever words need to pour onto the page. Eat—best of all, cook for yourself—something you really love to eat. Take a long bath or shower. Get lost in a book. Breathe. The world will get by fine.

Don't discard sleep

It's ridiculous how much difference something so straightforward as getting enough sleep can make to your well-being. You can even lose weight every year if you substitute an hour of TV watching for an hour of sleep each night. Getting enough sleep will improve your health, reduce your risk of disease, help you cope with anything stressful, and lift your mood.

For one month, try winding down to quieter activities an hour and a half earlier and going to bed an hour earlier at night. Compare how you feel, physically and mentally, at the beginning and end of the month. You may never go back to cutting short your zzzs again!

While you're at it, though, don't stress too much about nighttime wakefulness. It's totally normal for humans, according to Virginia Tech University sleep historian Roger Ekirch (as cited by Natalie Wolchover in *LifeScience*). Regard it as "segmented sleep" instead of "insomnia." Relax, and use those moments for quiet activities: think deep thoughts, fantasize, meditate, and enjoy doing nothing for a bit until your body is ready for sleep again.

You have permission not to run yourself into the ground

Go slow. Be kind, especially to yourself. Unknot your knots. Recognize that life is a marathon—not a sprint—and create regular distraction-free times to restore your energy, calm, and focus. Those with a romantic partner can do some of this sort of thing for each other but by no means all. Everyone—even those in a relationship—needs to be his or her own sweetheart from time to time. No one knows what we like best better than we do ourselves. Take time out—five minutes now, an hour later today, four hours within a week, a week within six months. Re-creation is vital!

Preparing for a real vacation

Can you take a week off? Can it be done without coming back to even more stress-inducing chaos than from which you escaped? *Yes!* Here are some tips that apply particularly to vacations, but which also illustrate helpful principles for having great weekends and better Monday mornings.

Clear your head before you head out on vacation. Schedule at least an hour a week with yourself in the three weeks before you leave to do the following:

- Brainstorm about all your open projects, deadlines and other stuff on your mind. Write it down as you go, either freeform or in a sketch or diagram style like a mind map, if you like something more visual.

- Look over your calendar for the months before, during, and after your time out of the office to spark recollection of any other open activities.

- Once you feel like your head is clear, group the things you wrote down into goals and projects. Identify the next actions in each of them and the date by which they must be done. If the deadline is before your trip, then schedule a day to do them. If it's during or in the week after, do them early or delegate them. If they're due more than a week after but less than a month after, list them in a clear, prioritized way on a piece of paper, and set that front and center on your desk as your starting point for your return.

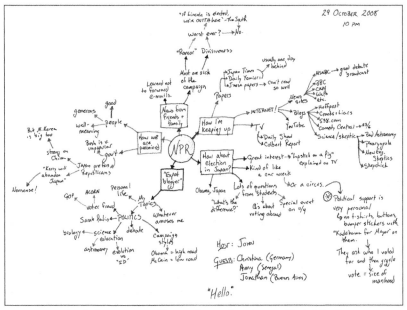

A mind map created by teacher and podcaster Chris Gladis
to focus his thoughts before a 2005 radio appearance.
(Used by permission. CC by-nd.)

- Briefly talk over at a high level the status, next actions, and upcoming deadlines for your active projects with your boss and colleagues who may cover for you while you're gone. If they'll need to cover a lot of new ground in your absence, provide them with a similar sheet listing next steps, goals and deadlines for that project.

- Place a clearly marked inbox on your chair or desk to receive papers and physical objects that come to you while you're out.

You'll be able to travel knowing that nothing is forgotten—you gave yourself three whole weeks to remember anything known—and you've prepared others to deal with unknowns within the context of your goals.

It also helps to return from long vacations on a Wednesday and use Thursday to recombobulate at home and finish unpacking. Then, spend Friday on processing email and, if you quietly sneak into the office, any accumulated inbox papers. Say to everyone that you'll be back in the office on Monday, but use Friday to get yourself soundly back on your feet at work, with a weekend as an additional reward for doing so!

A business travel variant on this trick is not to fly back the day a big conference ends, but instead fly home the next afternoon or evening. Ask the front desk at your hotel for late checkout so you can take your morning as slowly as you want. Then leave your bags at the desk and go putter around, have a nice lunch somewhere, and see something you might have otherwise missed. Give yourself a little breathing room to internalize the value of your travels.

Returning with a fresh perspective

Before you dive back into your inboxes, give yourself the gift of an hour or two of high-level, undistracted, newly relaxed thinking about your work, tools and processes. Pull back for the big picture since travel has already provided with you a little distance. Look at your space with fresh eyes. Have a large trash can and some archiving boxes brought to your workspace and purge stuff that is not currently useful, required, or inspiring. This kind of strategic time can be hard to carve out of day-to-day business, so take this opportunity for quality thinking.

Think about your roles and responsibilities:

- Where do you repeatedly need to be applying your focus and energy?

- Are you currently in a period of growth or stability or stagnation?

- Are you routinely giving yourself the clarity to have the answer to the question, "Where do I stand?"

- What's the next thing you need to learn?

- With whom do you need to build a connection?

- How are you communicating your values and priorities to prime others for your future decisions and actions?

Once you have a better understanding of what's going on at those high levels, you can descend into looking at specific goals—the waymarkers on your journey. Consider where you want to be in a week, a month, six months, and a year from now. Think about your current strategic position and where it should be at each of those points. Identify the feedback mechanisms that will tell you how things are going.

Clarity on the highest levels of what you want for yourself can reveal goals that are no longer valid for you. That's fine. Not all goals are equally important; some you'd regret on your deathbed if they weren't completed, but most you wouldn't even remember. Don't get stressed out over the latter as if they were the former.

———

With goals in order, you can turn to the active projects on which you're moving forward at least every week or two. Consider how many active projects for which you actually have time *at the moment* if you're going to be successful with any of them.

Decide on what you want or need to be working now and confirm that all of the projects on your list are really about you and what you should be doing. Be sure to include creative, artistic, or fun projects on your list to keep a good balance in your life. Consider your inactive projects long enough to confirm that the right stuff is getting your attention and swap active and inactive status on projects as necessary.

———

At this point, you are ready to get down to the specific tasks, which are the steps in completing these projects. It's easy to spend most of our days down in the trenches putting together the components of our bigger ideas. When you return from a vacation, take advantage of your higher perspective to see the whole landscape and confirm that the details are still in line with the blueprint for yourself.

———

Some last things to contemplate while you're looking at the big picture: are "roadblocks" and "tools."

Are you facing roadblocks right now? Anything hanging you up, actually or mentally? You can often tease out the answers to this question by considering what problem you most want solved this week, what interferes the most with working on your top priorities, and what work you most dread. Sometimes the roadblocks take the form of barriers to trust, collaboration, commitment, or success within a team. Reframe those problems as projects and find actions that you can take to reduce that barrier.

Do you have the tools and processes you need for sustainable success? Look at how you track what needs to be done for your active projects, what you may want to do later on inactive projects, and how you get the inactive stuff out of your head so you can focus on the active. Examine the method by which you decide what to do next and bring it closer to flowing naturally from your big-picture decisions instead of just being whatever falls into your lap because it's quick and easy, next in your calendar or inbox, the pet topic of a squeaky wheel, or the most stale. Take the temperature on where your time goes and keep it in the hot zone of your top priorities.

———

Now choose the next five actions that will drive forward what is most important and write them down.

———

Calmly, without beating yourself up, think back on some things that went wrong or were not as you'd hoped. Find common patterns and brainstorm on how those patterns can start to change. In all this relaxed thinking, and with the knowledge that the world didn't stop turning while you were on vacation, see if you've uncovered something you could start delegating, a meeting that you no longer need to attend or could make shorter or less frequent.

———

Lastly, from this point of perspective, ask yourself if there is anything about which you've been caring that doesn't fit in; if so, give yourself permission to stop caring about that. Maybe it's a dream you've dropped, something that really ought to be parked on a someday-maybe list (or crossed off of one), or an obstacle that's nonexistent or insignificant on which it's time to stop fixating needlessly.

What do you do on vacation that you would enjoy doing a little bit every week? Find something unrewarding to cut, and replace that with your favorite soul-restoring time. For many people, it is sitting down and losing yourself in a book for a while. Wall off some time to feed your stock of ideas.

Take a deep breath and remember yourself in this mental space of clear perception. The next time things get crazy—and after a vacation it often can come fast—remember that you have the capability to get back here.

Vacation lessons year round: precuperate

Preparing isn't only a useful trick when leaving town. You can take the opportunity to "precuperate" at any time to make the following week easier. Any of the following actions can make a big difference in the days ahead:

- Pick out your clothes for the next day and make sure you have enough clean things to get you through the workweek.

- If you had to get up early or aren't feeling 100%, take a little nap before sundown—just a catnap to give you a little extra rest.

- Make sure you have all the groceries you need in order to eat well throughout the week.

- Pack a good lunch for tomorrow.

- Set out the breakfast things before you go to bed so it's easy to fuel up at the start of the day.

- Do something fun and silly—laughter is great medicine!

- Take a little time to be still, do nothing at all, and let your mind lose its busy buzzing.

The Look-Ahead

Life is full of surprises, but there are plenty of things that stress us out that we could have predicted and made less painful if we'd only planned a little bit. You can dramatically reduce your craptastic moments by following the simple practice of regularly doing the six simple steps of The Look-Ahead.

1. Look at what's coming up on your calendar and to-do list.

2. Think about what you'll need to make it go right and about what could go wrong.

3. Learn from the recent past by recalling what was less than optimal during that time.

4. Think about how you could avoid or reduce similar hassles in the future.

5. Implement as many of those positive changes as possible.

6. Confirm that you have properly noted any preparatory to-do's on your list, especially anything that requires an errand.

It's so simple, but we all see people failing to do this, like that guy at the Department of Motor Vehicles, who is having a hissy fit because he's been waiting in line and didn't bring anything with him to turn that time into something productive or enjoyable. Don't be that guy. How about that gal, who is running all over town on her lunch break and trying to find a present for a birthday party she's attending right after work tonight? Don't be that gal. It's really not hard to steer yourself clear of a lot of pain.

Once a month, have everyone in your household sit down with their calendars and quickly go over the next six and the past six weeks, making sure that every event impacting other people is known and learning what works well. Everyone should know houseguests are coming, when they need to give someone else a ride or otherwise be available, or about similar significant features in the domestic landscape.

Once a week, do The Look-Ahead with your work and personal calendars for the next and past month. On what would you like to look back a month from now and know that you did? What loose ends from the past month do you need to tie off?

At the end of each day, look ahead for the next morning, noting commitments and writing down anything from now that you want to pick up again then.

Set yourself up for happy calm. It won't always work, but it's worth it when it does.

Slow down

A large part of keeping yourself happy boils down to slowing down long enough to pay attention to what you need. Eat lightly and blandly if your belly is weary. Drink water if your head is aching. Sleep more if you're tired. Be alone if you're weary of people; if you're not, be with those who give you energy rather than drain it. Take whatever forms of rest you need. Stop not being awesome to yourself. You have the right to be completely selfish sometimes—and, in truth, it is necessary in order to be able to give more and better over time. Slow down, cool down, and be your best.

As clinical psychologist Ester Buchholz said, "Others inspire us, information feeds us, practice improves our performance, but we need quiet time to figure things out, to emerge with new discoveries, to unearth original answers."

———

Discardia reminds us to let go of our hurry and listen for what we can do to make our lives better.

25 Distraction

Be Here Now

> When someone is impatient and says, "I haven't got
> all day," I always wonder, How can that be?
> How can you not have all day?
> — *George Carlin, comedian and social critic*

Acting, not reacting

Living in a hurried state of mind dilutes your physical senses as well as your senses of place and self. Continually skimming over things in a rush, without taking time to consider, can push you into a state where stopping creates anxiety. Could humans have designed tools more perfect for that ceaseless motion than the Internet, email, and microblogging services like Twitter? Breaking free from that state of connection—a kind of "disconnection from contemplation"—means pushing through the discomfort of adjustment when you stop.

As process artist, teacher, and social technologies facilitator Chris Corrigan marveled, "Amazing how deep the mindset goes, how infected we are by craving, acquisition and the perpetually postponed present."

If you step back from the datastream to think, suddenly you aren't moving on to the next blip of input. Instead of being pulled forward wherever it leads, you are faced with choosing your direction. You thwart your expectation of knowing what comes next and of receiving something to which you can react. Suddenly nothing is steering you. What should you do?

Stop distracting yourself and decide what matters right now, and then do that. Know the problem you want to solve or the improved state of the world you want to create. Ask yourself, "What is the outcome I am seeking?" I've heard GTD coaches phrase this as "What would done look like?" Knowing what to do next depends a good deal on where you want to get to, so make the time to identify your dreams, goals, and projects.

> Start your mornings right. Before email or voicemail, jot down your three top priority tasks today. Scan those inputs very quickly to see if anything else bumps up to (and knocks something out of) the top three, but do at least one of those three before anything else.

Learn to listen

Simple, right? Nope. This one is a lot harder than it seems and critical to success in all aspects of life. Shut up—mouth and mind and distractions—and really listen. Then think. *Then* respond or act. Ask questions, clarify, confirm. Even when you're working on something for yourself, 10 minutes spent unpacking and spelling out your expectations in writing or aloud can both vastly improve the finished work and steer you clear of avoidable problems.

Look with fresh eyes at self-distraction sources. What has more prominence than it deserves? Turn off the alerts for what you will check anyway. Stop interrupting yourself needlessly. Multitasking is an illusion; the best you can do is to switch tasks quickly and get back in the flow rapidly with each change.

To be more productive and rewarded, don't try to do more at once; instead, choose your actions well and do what you are doing with greater focus. You will achieve more when working on multiple projects if you give them your full attention for set chunks of time than if you incessantly flit between them. The chunks don't need to be very large—even 15- to 30-minute laps can be hugely productive for many activities. Focus and don't give in to the "I'll just take a quick peek to see if there's new email" urges as you work. (If you need a little help with your willpower, try LeechBlock (a Firefox browser extension) to limit your work-time visiting of nonwork websites.)

When you're creating or connecting, shut down other inputs. Turn off chat and message services when writing email or blog posts. Turn the TV off during conversation. Clean all the icons off your computer desktop that do not lead to the tasks you're doing today. Group short-cuts together in a toolbar or dock and set your system to hide it when you aren't using it. A clear desktop on your computer allows it to take its natural role as a workbench, always ready for the project at hand.

Do the same with your physical space. Ask yourself, "When my desk helps me do my best work, what *isn't* here?" Create an environment to encourage yourself to focus and to relax. Headphones sure help tune out distractions in an open-plan office!

Cut the noise

The principle of hiding options you aren't currently using can apply out-side of the desk environment, too. Next time you're in a hotel, reduce the visual noise by stashing all those little stand-up signs and promotion cards in a drawer. You deserve a space that is not covered in ads or obses-sive admonitory notes. Make your surroundings harmonize with what you're there to do.

Where does the time go?

I highly doubt that anyone seeking a less cluttered life is someone who finds too much time on their hands. So where is all your time going? Put up a piece of paper where you'll keep seeing it, such as on the fridge or next the computer. Then, all week write down where your time goes each day (e.g., "90 minutes reading blogs," "30 minutes cooking dinner," "110 minutes commuting," "10 hours working," "25 minutes for lunch," or "11 hours watching TV").

There's even software to help with this act of observation while you're at your keyboard. Check out RescueTime, which works on both Macs and Windows computers. At the end of the week, compare what you did to what you wish you were doing. What's the biggest chunk of time invested for the least payoff? What could you completely or mostly eliminate and then replace with something more important to you?

Cut out the low-return stuff. Not quit cold turkey, but cut out, snip away at, and remove bit by bit. Focus on these two things to change:

1. A mental habit or worry, which is eating too much of your energy or time; and

2. A project or routine, which isn't going anywhere or which distracts you from things on which you wish you'd spend more time.

Swap time that doesn't reward you for time that does.

What do you love?

Have you made what you love as obvious to you as whatever else eats up your time? Get those better options in front of you. If you magically had no obligations for three days, such as no lost opportunities or work piled up when you came back and no expectations of you, how would you spend that time? Work that into your days now. Whatever you choose, do something that makes your life happier than whatever activity is at the bottom of that mindless rut into which you keep falling. Stay amused under your own power. You'll find yourself more energized than by consuming virtual junk food.

Don't channel-surf or link-hop just because you want something but haven't figured out what it is. Your time is finite. It matters how you spend it.

Certainly, you can consciously decide that what you really want to do is flip around getting mental stimulation and enjoying it whole-heartedly. I'm betting, though, that everyone has chunks of time spent on autopilot—and not autopilot in the useful "my mind is happily wandering while I vacuum" sense, but in the sense of failing to select that which will reward us somehow. Be where you are, doing what you're doing and enjoy it as much as you can.

Tune in to the good stuff

The rewards of focus come not only with work—whether for yourself or others—but in all aspects of life. Be more aware of what you are doing and the doing gets better. Put on some favorite music, head into the kitchen and throw together some pasta and sauce with fresh ingredients instead of robotically warming up a frozen dinner. Walk to the park and back instead of driving to the gym and trudging on a treadmill. When there's no need for mental walls, take out your earbuds and listen to where you are instead of muffling your surroundings in a protective coating of music. Perceive.

> Here's a nice Saturday morning routine you might want to start: Get up and have a little breakfast. Pour a cup of your favorite morning beverage and head out to your front stoop with the broom. Shake the doormat, pick up any trash about the place, and sweep up the dirt. If you live in an apartment building, this could just be sweeping a bit around your door and the path you take to the stairs or elevator, but I recommend even in that case going down to the street door and sweeping the sidewalk. It doesn't take long, it makes a place you see every day nicer, and it gives you a chance to say hello to your neighbors. Urban and suburban lives are often far more isolated than is healthy, either for the people who live that way or the neighborhood as a whole. Get to know at least the faces and better yet, some names.

Whether it's checking in with the life of your neighborhood and the season or opening yourself up to more mindful work, set aside distractions and be here now. Open your eyes and see something you've been ignoring. Clear away a stale stack of papers on your desk. Knock away the next half hour of to-dos on a procrastinated project. Acknowledge a truth. Learn about a country about which you know nothing. Write or draw whatever is on your mind. Connect with someone you like and with someone you love to remind them that they rock; someday you won't have the chance to do so again.

Celebrate the simple miracles in your life and give yourself the best opportunities and surroundings to enjoy them. How many excellent things can you allow to fall into your life in the next 24 hours? Start counting the delights. *Carpe diem!*

26

Plugged into the Wrong Connections

Unfollow-Unsubscribe-Cancel-Delete-Donate-Discard

> It used to be you define yourself by what you use;
> now you define yourself by what you don't use.
> —*Kevin Kelly, editor*

What's coming at you?

As you shift your habits to spend more time on what is truly important to you, it will also be necessary to adjust how much of that important stuff you can actually take on without creating new stresses for yourself. Even though you're doing the right things to reduce your load, it can seem as if you're still only able to make so much progress before you get that drowning feeling again. That's when you need to stop setting yourself up for the backlogged life.

What floodgates have you opened onto yourself under which you're currently standing, complaining about how wet you are? Certainly technology is partly to blame for the problem. As Greg Knauss pointed out, "The tools I use to manage information have evolved to the point where I can abdicate the tedious process of gathering it all together to them, and they now do a very diligent job of making sure that it's all brought to my attention. Endlessly. Maddeningly."

We live under an avalanche of voicemail, email, TiVo recommendations, feed reader and social network posts, magazines, catalogs, Twitter links, charity solicitations, books, as well as all of the other to-dos we give ourselves.

To escape you can take the radical Move It or Lose It approach and discard everything older than a certain date; however, for most of us, that's a bit too bold. Instead, we can increase the efforts we've already started—reducing the incoming stream and processing that stream more quickly—while adding a new element, "completion by deletion."

In GTD terms, we can start dropping a lot of things that would otherwise go on our someday-maybe lists. Here's the rationale: That magical day—when we're caught up on the things higher on the list (either in priority or urgency or both) and get to this stuff—will never come. We are never going to get down to the someday-maybe stuff by eliminating everything above it.

It's not "next in line"; it's a parking lot for ideas we might want to reconsider sometime. To do those things, they have to climb back out of that low level and catch our attention again. If they become important or urgent, they will. So pare down your inactive projects list and remove anything about which you no longer care if you forget forever. Then, later, if you're all caught up, you can add it back (or not).

Create your forcefield

Choose the inputs that you want to receive—not just what is flung your direction but of what you want to be aware. Realize that you've got an attention force field, through which you can allow only some things to come. Email is one of them, but under your terms (e.g., the settings you choose and your spam filters). You are in charge of these inputs to your life; you can't control the content, but you can control their impact on your attention.

Pull back from the infostream. Imagine a quality filter designed just for you. Think about how it would simplify your life if you only (or at least mostly) received what is relevant to your interests. What would it let through? What would it exclude? How would you like it to balance receiving that which you *enjoy* getting with receiving enough of what you *need* to get, even if it isn't always fun?

When you re-engage, unfollow what you imagined your filter would eliminate. Fine-tune—even, perhaps especially, from the lists you create for yourself. As Mark Hurst said in *Bit Literacy*, "Know what you consume, and why, and be strict about evaluating what else to consume, especially online."

Say "no" more often. Remember: You don't have to finish everything you think of starting or keep up with everything anyone else does. Review your to-do lists and cross off anything that is unimportant, nonurgent, and which will remind you of itself later if you wind up really needing or wanting to do it. That last bit is important: As of today, redefine your to-do list as "Things I Need to Think About This Week." If you can totally ignore an item for a couple of weeks, it belongs on your calendar, should be filed away with a future scheduled project, put on your someday-maybe list, or allowed to slip away. If it matters, it will come back.

Prune the backlog

Do some thinking about what comes into your life and creates a backlog. Decide what you can live without— and live more happily. What return are you getting on your investment of time, energy, and focus? Would something else pay off better either now or in the long term? Shift to that.

If the backlog awaiting your attention isn't pressuring you, that's excellent; however, when it does, try some of these ideas:

Consider canceling your Netflix subscription and not using TiVo's recommendation feature. For many, what matters most about their Netflix account is the queue—a someday-maybe list of movies to watch—so just keep the list if you're not keeping up with incoming films. Take that subscription money (or saved late fees if you've been renting from a traditional video store or library) and put 80% of it into savings. Invest the rest in really good chocolate. I bet you'll take care of *that* tonight!

Use CatalogChoice.org. Slow that cascade of advertising dripping from your mailbox.

Contemplate canceling or reducing magazine and newspaper subscriptions—at least abandon any feeling of obligation that you have to read the whole thing. Recycle all the half-read ones lying around—or put them on 48-hour warning and then recycle them. Observe your information flow. How many come in per week? How many do you read? Adjust the inflow accordingly.

If you still have more than one phone, live with only one voice-mail box. That nagging blinking light shouldn't be the first thing to greet you when you get home or pick up your cellphone.

Consider unsubscribing from all, most, or at least many of your email lists, digital newsletters, and feed-reader subscriptions. Imagine if you printed all those saved mailing list posts, downloaded articles, and feed subscriptions. How big a stack would you have? Don't make your computer the digital version of one of those people's houses where you have to edge around on goat trails between teetering piles of moldering news. Be realistic about the amount of time you spend "keeping up with sites." Pick a reasonable number based on your available time and about how much of it you want to spend online. Visit the others when they come to mind.

If you forget to check a site, it's not that important. Find your balance and let go of the rest. My friend, online community consultant Heather Champ, created her own "Project Unsubscribe" when she set out to make her email inbox feel more like a living room and less like a strip mall. After a few months, when the pace of her unsubscriptions slowed down, she had stopped almost 300 newsletters and unnecessary notifications. Her verdict? "Inbox quality A+++."

Unrewarding is unrewarding; prune your follow lists and subscriptions with blithe abandon when it comes to social media and newsletters.

Prune physical piles of reading materials that are nagging you. Where in your week have you allocated time for that reading? Match expectation to opportunity and vice versa.

Here's how to make the unread less daunting. Put on some good music and sit down next to the piles of books (and magazines and clipped articles) with three boxes named the following:

1. Ooh! Inticing!

2. Hmm, I think I want to read this.

3. Do I have to read this?

When you're tired of sorting into those three categories, tidy up by putting the #3 stuff in your charity, sell, recycling, or to-be-returned spots as appropriate. Then put the #2 stuff out of the way (e.g., in a basket behind your comfy chair or under the coffee table). Last, put the #1 stuff in spots where you like to have something at hand to read and reward yourself now with a little reading time with whatever catches your eye.

If your unread books make you feel guilty, don't buy books unless you're going to start reading them within the next 48 hours. Ann Arbor Discardian John Hritz took that kind of approach: "I've gone zero-sum or less on books, CDs, DVDs, clothes, etc. By zero-sum, I mean that to buy one, I donate one or more. This gets me out of the binge and purge mentality of organizing. I try to have a place in mind for something I want to buy and if there's already something there it has to go."

If it's really getting to you to see that stack and putting the yet-to-be-read in a less prominent location doesn't relieve your feelings of obligation, eliminate all but two of the things in your read-next pile—loan 'em to someone, donate 'em to the library, sell 'em, whatever—but eliminate the reading guilt.

Consolidate your personal email. Do you have more than one personal email account or more than one email program with a pile of saved or unread mail in it? Think about each of them. What if it suddenly went away? Would you be sad or would you shrug? If the former, find a way to extract the important messages, forward them to your current account and archive them or otherwise make a backup; if the latter, decide why you are rewarded by still having that account or get rid of it.

———

Every time you feel guilty over optional inputs with which you aren't dealing, treat that as a reminder to eliminate 10 things taking up your time, energy, or space. Suppose that you had a magic free 20 minutes. Which unread magazine is the last one you'd pick up? Cancel that subscription. Which unread book? Donate it. Unfollow-unsubscribe-cancel-delete-donate-discard.

Tune your tech

Use the tech that brings you value and use it in a way that brings value to the people with whom you use it. Twitter is good for keeping in touch, but be sure to populate your list of friends you follow with only those whose updates you really want to see. You don't have to get updates sent to your phone or instant-messaging client. As a quick thermometer of what a group of people is doing, Twitter is a nice service—brief, frequently silly, ignorable as necessary.

If Twitter isn't for you, you can or are probably getting a similar effect from your Facebook or Google+ or Flickr contacts or blog post titles in a feed reader. Bottom line: Just because you're friends, it doesn't mean that you're obligated to keep up with the entirety of each other's electronic output.

Edward Vielmetti encapsulated this nicely: "You can only deal with so much interruption in a day, and if the channels you are tuned into have too much static, remove some of the static."

We are biologically attuned to changes in our environment, so be very wary of what you allow to light up with a red flag, sound a bell, or otherwise poke you. Go for quality over quantity. You should also consider the quality of your own output. Vielmetti had a tip there as well: "It can be instructive from time to time to tune in to your own electronic output and see what kind of droppings you are leaving behind—there is certainly a balance and moderation between tell-all and hermit for each one of us."

Examine your output as if you were the recipient you least want to offend and most want to win over. Is it clear, concise, and well formatted? Share the good stuff, in the right amount, or, as Merlin Mann put it, "You want to see the web as a party where you bring more beer than you drink."

Connect selectively

No matter what the latest "information overload" panic piece in the news may be telling us, we *do* have the power to control this and don't need to be broadsided by it. Technologist and long-time blogger Tom Coates translated all the hype for us: "Shock revelation! A new set of technologies has started to displace older technologies and will continue to do so at a fairly slow rate over the next ten to thirty years!" Put it like that and it doesn't seem so hard to handle, does it?

We have lots of options in this world and that's not unexpected or bad; what gets us in trouble is not choosing among them. Be selective about what you want or need to know. Opt out of communication that doesn't make you feel more like yourself, make your day better, or teach you something you need to learn now.

27

Making Nice

Integrity (Integrated)

> If you're not careful time will take away everything
> that ever hurt you, everything you have ever lost,
> and replace it with knowledge.
> —*Charles Yu, author*

Draw the line

My dad gave me some good advice: "Getting what we do, and what we say, and what we feel to be about the same is my definition of integrity—integrated—and that is more important than being fair, nice, moral, etc."

Always be honest with yourself and as much of the time as possible with others. If your gut strongly says "no" to something, find a way to not to have your mouth say "yes." At the very least, give yourself options with a qualified "yes."

Let that overdedicated knitter know that, though you love the fact that he takes the time to make you something special, you never seem to wear anything handknit, or else suggest a garment within his skill range that you would wear. When someone asks for help with something and you can tell already that it's going to snowball into a giant chore, set some limits up front (e.g., "I'm pretty booked right now, but I could give you two hours of help one weekday evening between now and the 15th.").

Set boundaries for the fun but demanding things. Try bold, new adventures and push yourself in creative ways. Participate in National Novel Writing Month. Try out new crafts. Make improvements on your home. Start up a topical blog. Keep your expectations fun by placing limits (e.g., "I'll do this for 30 days," "I'll drop the class if I'm not liking it for the third session in a row," "I'll see if I can do this beginner's project, which is supposed to take about four hours," or "I'll replace the curtains, and then think about the rest of the remodeling after I see how that goes").

Pair big goals with quick wins

When you're going to work on something that's new or tough, here's a technique that can increase your odds of success. Try balancing the big goal with some small secondary ones in the same territory. They'll keep you motivated through the long haul on the big goal as you accomplish the easier ones. Though you may not completely change that big situation, you'll feel good to have checked a couple things off your list along with making a bit of progress by whittling away at the harder goal.

Enrichment

Silicon Valley entrepreneur, author and speaker Rajesh Setty suggested steps that to me epitomize the integrated life:

- **Commit:** Commit to lifetime-relationships that span events, companies, causes and geographic boundaries.

- **Care:** Care for the concerns of others as if they are your own.

- **Connect:** Aim to connect those who will benefit and enrich each other's lives in equal measure.

- **Communicate:** Communicate candidly. Tell people what they should hear rather than what they want to hear.

- **Expand Capacity:** Aim to expand people's capacity to help them give and get more from their own lives.

As you help others, know that they don't have to go it alone; remember to give yourself that gift, too. Make time to be around people you love. Even if it's just for a quick cup of coffee and commiseration, or 20 minutes on the phone in the middle of a hectic week, take a drink from that well of affection and friendship and support.

Diversify your emotional support portfolio

It's a good idea to have more than one supportive well to help sustain you. Even enormously personal and deep things can change, and some friends may not be ready for that difference right away or ever. Fully follow your values, even when it means as profound a shift as discarding your affiliation with the church in which you've been for six decades.

Former president and human rights worker Jimmy Carter took that significant step when he left the Southern Baptist Convention because they do not recognize the fundamental equality of women. It takes incredible courage to let go of a bias with which you were raised and to step away from a community of support, but sometimes it is the only way to grow and to teach.

There is an anecdote in business lore in which the chief financial officer says to the chief executive officer, "What happens if we invest in developing our people and they leave us?" The CEO replies, "What happens if we don't, and they stay?"

What happens if you invest in who you really are and it changes everything? What happens if you don't and nothing changes?

Accept the finite

As ripe as the future may seem, the true potential is in the present. That is when we need to act to take our lives in the direction we want to go. At some point, your days of having choices will run out. Someone else is going to decide for you. That's the lesson I learned cleaning out my grandmother's apartment when her health failed and she moved into a nursing home. Somebody will be whittling down everything you own to the essentials. Perhaps you'll be lucky and that person will know you well or will be following your instructions, but, one way or another, you'll get the big reminder that we are not immortal.

Our time in this world is brief so spend it where it matters to you and not where it doesn't. Make a commitment to give yourself a life that brings you more satisfaction. What could our days be like if we focus more on what really matters to us and carve away, patiently, inexorably, that which blocks us from being who we want to be? If this stuff doesn't really matter when we pare our lives down to the essentials, why do we choose to clutter our homes and minds with it until then? Why bury the truly important stuff beneath all this fluff?

The truly important stuff

Love life and your friends fiercely. If you have to let go of everything else to get a good hold on this, do it.

Care. Madly, passionately.

Be yourself. There's no such thing as "larger than life"; be fully alive and present and true. It doesn't get more important than that.

Laugh. Loud, long, often.

Smile. Get other people to do it, too.

Be kind. Randomly, bewilderingly, unexpectedly, sweetly.

Keep being inspired by those who've made your world better.

———

One of the most decent people I know, MetaFilter community creator Matt Haughey, said, "It sounds simple and trite but the most important thing seems to be just living a life with joy in it. Bonus if filled with joy."

Nothing is stopping you from doing something good and true, be it small or big.

Part Four

December Discardia: Core Principle #3— Perpetual Upgrade

20/20 hindsight

When Discardia comes around in December on that shortest day—the winter solstice—celebrate by releasing yourself from a self-imposed deadline and giving thanks for what is good in the world. In addition, let this also be the season of giving yourself what you need to be truly joyful and just plain happy.

Look back on your year and see how things compare to last December. Recognize and enjoy the improvements you've made in your world.

- What has provided you with the most satisfaction?

- Can you do more in that area to provide a similar payoff?

This is the season to say thanks to yourself. Seek out the right choices you've made in the past year, great and small, and acknowledge your good sense in curing those causes of dissatisfaction.

You have a supportive framework of good habits, can see the rewards of your decisions and what you did about them, and have replaced some of your less exciting quantity with energizing quality. Now it's time to turn up the volume on the awesomeness and build the habit of upgrading your experiences.

Think back on your past:

- What did you learn from good but not ideal apartments, jobs, and relationships?

- Are there patterns or antipatterns that point you in the direction of positive change in your life today?

Add this question to your mental toolbox: "What does this look like when it works?" You can apply that to any functional object, space, time, or relationship that is currently less than ideal.

This mindset leads to other good questions. For example:

- What do I want to see (and not see) when I walk in the front door?

- What is bedtime like when it leads me into a great night's sleep?

- What would a good mentor provide me now?

Give that part of your world a nudge in the right direction.

———

First step: Do better than just survive December.

28

Holiday Stress

Freedom from Obligation is the Best Gift

> I've reached that peculiar but serene stage in life
> when all I want for Christmas is less.
> —*Roger Ebert, writer and critic*

The weight of the season

Even the luckiest of us feel a bit of extra pressure around the end of the year. In a 2006 survey by the American Psychological Association (APA) over half of respondents reported that they often or sometimes experience stress, irritability, and/or fatigue during the holidays, with the leading stressors being lack of time, lack of money, and commercialism or hype (in contrast to work and money, which lead at other times of year).

It's not just Christmas. The whole season is enough to make anyone rebel against all that pressure. I'm not the only one to invent holidays out of that stress: Buy Nothing Day and Festivus owe their origins to some of the same forces that launched Discardia. From the moment we lock the front door on Halloween night and poke through the leftover trick-or-treat candy, we jump into a wild, obligation-ridden bobsled run, whisking us through Thanksgiving, Christmas, and New Year's Eve, until we're dumped headfirst into the cold, slushy snow of the first bleak week of January.

We feel the whirlwind begin as ads suggest "the perfect gift for the such and such on your list." This list is assumed; of course, everyone has a list. Everyone must be buying. Post-turkey Friday comes and the retail frenzy begins. The crowds and the sensory overload of enforced commercial festivity. "Bring on the cheer, *dammit!*" seems to be the underlying message of the barrage of Christmas music, holiday movie promotions, and red and green advertising plastered on every surface. Sometimes it seems like you couldn't throw a rock without hitting a Santa—and, as December barrels on, the temptation to do so grows.

Let's not forget the family pressures. Whether anyone in your own family applies it, pop culture is more than ready to step in with the traditional holiday guilt. "Welcome to December! Here's your script. You know your part. It's magic time! As our sponsor would like to remind you, magic means presents, so shop 'til you drop! Charge it! After all, doesn't your family *deserve* a joyous holiday season?"

Friends and families gather together for whatever holidays they celebrate. Events are planned with all their special rituals, running the gamut from two separate kinds of cranberry sauce for differing tastes right up to Midnight Mass and *Auld Lang Syne* in Times Square. People are pulled from their normal surroundings—or worse, have to tidy them up for an onslaught of visitors—and are forced to do particular things at particular times, always a potential source of stress.

There is no time of year more likely to run people ragged than the holidays. All the pressure to set the perfect holly jolly scene makes family tensions worse than ever. I don't know about your financial state of affairs, but I don't come to the end of the year thinking, "Wow! Look at all this extra money! I think I'll buy a bunch of stuff." Like me, you've probably experienced pressure to overspend at this time of year and had a lean winter paying it all back.

It's optional

I am here to tell you that holiday gift buying is *optional*. It is possible to have a happy family gathering without breaking the bank. You can have a blessed season without shattering your peace of mind. You can make it the season of giving without it being the season of shopping.

You don't have to buy all those presents. *Really.* Most people don't need more stuff and no one needs more debt. Indeed, in that same 2006 APA survey 47% of respondents cited the pressure of giving *or getting* gifts as something that causes them stress. (If you're having trouble thinking of why receiving gifts would be stressful, spend a few minutes browsing whydidyoubuymethat.com and you'll remember.)

Why put ourselves through this? Most of us in the First World have so much stuff that a pile of presents is no longer exciting or novel. There are lots of alternatives to the holiday shopping madness and many other ways to remind people that you care about them. Something for the kids, sure, but you don't have to break the bank to spread that holiday cheer.

Alternatives to over-gifting

First and foremost, tell them you care. Write them a note, call them on the phone, bump into them at the grocery store—whatever—but just say, "You know, I am so glad to have you in my life." Maybe suggest a get-together, perhaps after the holidays when things aren't so busy. Even if you only let them know that you appreciate them, you can be giving something much greater than a hastily selected present.

When you do want to give a gift, there are many kinds that won't strain your credit or leave you frazzled:

Cooked things that you actually enjoy making. My friend, librarian Kristin Garrity, makes the most wonderful holiday cookies, but the best part is the conversation we have while I'm nibbling on those tasty treats from her kitchen.

Homemade gift certificates for future fun together. I have had tremendous fun making up little books of these certificates for someone special. Each one becomes a shared dream of a good time I want us to have together. The words "A walk in the woods with the smell of damp earth and redwoods and the sound of the wind in the treetops" are already something special, made even better when you both make the time to make the dream real.

Mix CDs or playlists (of music or photos). I've been introduced to lots of great music and visuals this way, by both family and friends. Okay, maybe I wind up spending some of that money I saved on gifts buying the albums with a song I particularly liked; however, every time I hear that music, I think of the person who first shared their fondness for it with me.

Donations to charities (monetary or, if you have more hours than cash, your time in honor of someone else). My grandmother's tradition was to give us Heifer Project gifts, which meant that we got all the amusement of receiving a goat without the actual "goat in the house" part.

Memories. One year, my family "unwrapped" memories. Everyone took turns at telling a favorite memory of each other person. Those stories reminded us of what we treasure about each other and it was a lovely way to spend time together.

When gift giving, try to create an opportunity for the recipient rather than giving a thing. How can you free this person for joyful engagement?

Even low-stress families benefit from less holiday hoopla

I'm one of the lucky ones. My family is not by any stretch of the imagination a high-pressure one. Phrases like "Well, I need a little me time, so I'm going to go read for a bit" or "I think I'll take a nap" are often heard and accepted without causing tension.

As family holidays go, mine are awfully relaxing. Still, when I was a kid, Christmas was always a big deal for us. I grew up in a large house with high ceilings, and we took every advantage to make the holidays something special: a towering tree, covered in exotic ornaments; festive draperies; room for all the family to visit; and, of utmost interest to a little kid, lots of packages under that big tree. We had great big stockings, which could come up to your knee and which were bulging with fascinating things, for everyone—including the grownups—to open on Christmas morning.

The days leading up to Christmas proper were very exciting. On Christmas Eve, we each opened one package. On Christmas morning, everyone would gather—after digging into stockings upon waking—for the main opening of the presents, which was done one package at a time rather than en masse.

There were, as I said, a great many presents. So many, in fact, that in generous years (or in ones where many small gifts made up for few large ones), we would take a break in the process of opening them in order to have brunch and fortify ourselves. All this makes us sound fabulously wealthy; we were not. We just *liked* Christmas. For all the pleasures, though, it left us exhausted and broke.

Add up all the stuff—decorations, stockings, tree stands, draperies, strings of lights, and special plates for special meals—and we haven't even come to the presents themselves yet. At some point, my family began to see the forest instead of the Christmas trees. We realized that, despite all our rituals around the presents, our pleasure had almost nothing to do with the money that was spent, or even with the number of gifts.

We began to lower the pressure on ourselves and shift our focus to the less stress-inducing parts of the holiday. We started this by saying that everyone deserved one big present, but that we shouldn't all buy extras just to make sure that everyone got one. We decided to draw names so that we each knew for whom we were shopping for their big present. Drawing names worked very well and we transitioned from definitely buying something small for every person to only getting other gifts if particularly inspired.

As the number of presents declined, so did our stress levels in December. That turned out to be the nicest gift we could give each other. We began to have more energy and time for just being together on the holiday while cooking, talking, singing, reading aloud, and taking walks. Before many more years passed, we were down to a few presents each. The habit of opening a present on Christmas Eve faded and was replaced with experiential gifts to be shared, like a new jigsaw puzzle or a bunch of fancy cheeses to try. Now the presents are optional.

Our holiday memories are more—not less—rich for having fewer things involved in the season. Our homes are less cluttered, causing the chosen items we do keep to stand out and enrich our lives more easily. We remember and celebrate family and friends through digital pictures and stories, rather than objects, and our days are happier for it.

As I enter my holiday vacation time each year now, it's clear that the biggest gift my family has given each other is freedom from obligation.

The real gift and the real focus are being together. We have traded presents for presence.

No Home Position

29

A Room of One's Own

A house is a machine to live in and from which all
superfluous and irritating ornaments should be banished.
—*A. L. Sadler, professor of oriental studies*

Does your home support you in doing what you love?

As you focus on only the best parts of the holidays, take some time to
mull over what you love to do now and in general:

- Are you planning to get out and do some backpacking this year?
  Think about where you keep your equipment. If it's buried in the
  basement or the back of a closet, or scattered around the place,
  store it in a more convenient and organized way so you don't have
  a roadblock to getting out of town.

- Love to cook but your kitchen is a disaster area? Well, maybe it's
  time to run another quick lap and rid your kitchen of nonessentials. Reorganize if it will give you a better workspace. If you need
  to start the project of getting into a place with a better kitchen,
  figure out what you can do to set the stage for the life you want to
  be living.

Make a place for pleasures.

What qualities would you like your home to have?

Think back over the places you've lived. What was great about each of
them? What didn't you like and want to avoid in the future? Steadily

write these down until you're pretty sure that you have captured the most important stuff to you.

Now look it over.

- What do you have in your current place?

- What could you add here, or do you need to start thinking about a move to bring home more in line with your dreams? (Hot tip: When you're moving, create an upgrade list. You may not be able to afford the ideal version of something, but the fresh, critical eyes of a move bring the not-quite-there-yet stuff into focus.)

- What's the most important thing to you of the changes you want to make?

- What's the first step toward that? Write that down.

- What's the easiest thing? Do it right now if you can or arrange to do it as soon as possible.

Keep your list where you'll keep coming back to it regularly. Note: The list can change, just like you and that's fine. Move toward what matters to you now.

The room of rest

Go into your bedroom and see what pleases you and what doesn't. Are there things in there that don't belong? If so, figure out where they can move instead. If they can go nowhere else (hello, studio apartment dwellers!), could they be contained or disguised in a way to make them bother you less?

Are there things missing (for example, enough dresser space, an attractive laundry basket, or a rug by the bed to shield your morning toes from a cold floor)? Make a list and, if you have something on it that matters more to you in the bedroom then where it currently is, move it in right now. Would a different layout make you more comfortable and work better?

For those with larger places to live, consider whether you're using the right room for your bedroom. Thinking about the morning light can be helpful here. If another room might be better, play with the idea on paper and make some measurements before you start moving furniture. (Trust me on this one.)

Look at what you've set up for yourself as the last thing you see before you go to sleep and the first thing you see when you wake up:

- Has your bedside table become a cluttered mess?

- Are your surroundings generally unattractive?

- Are there nagging unfinished projects in view from your pillow?

Cut the clutter and tune your bedroom to reduce stress. If your bedside light is too bright or too dim or you are lacking one altogether and relying on an overhead light that doesn't soothe your senses, give yourself well-diffused lighting that's easy to turn off when you're ready to drift to sleep.

If you have all your potential and in-progress reading piled right beside the bed, tidy it up into a better holding location—perhaps in a very small bookcase—and keep only the active titles at arms' length. If you've got a jumble of remotes, could they go in a little basket or in a nightstand drawer instead? Better yet, have the TV leave the bedroom entirely and make this space more restful.

Think about what you really need to have right beside your bed and contain it appropriately in something pleasing to your senses. Give your room a feeling of rightness and comfort that will soothe you to sleep and refresh you when you wake. When you're dusting, sweeping, and vacuuming, start with your bedroom so it stays the cleanest place in the house. Allergies most definitely aren't relaxing.

At the least, find one thing you can do today to make you happier in your bedroom from now on. Sleeping better, waking, and starting your morning more calmly, and retiring to bed at the end of the evening to find a pleasant space that soothes your senses, all have a ripple effect that will positively influence your days.

Bring your living room to life

Think about the purposes of your living room, and then go in there and look at it with new eyes. Is it serving those purposes? What doesn't belong? Where else could it go? (Not the bedroom; you already decluttered that!) Move out of the way the things that hinder you from using this space. What's missing?

When I did this exercise some time ago, I realized that what I like is having friends over for meals and games. What I sorely needed was a table and enough chairs—the standing dinner party has never caught on for good reason. Fortunately, when I told one of my friends that I was thinking of going shopping for a good table, he said, "Oh, we have a great one in the basement and three chairs. They're yours!" Sometimes, all it takes is expressing a need for an opportunity to present itself. What would give your room what it needs to function well?

Could you rearrange things to better suit your favorite activities? If you like to sit and talk with people, have you arranged comfortable seating so that you are facing each other? Until recently, my current living room suffered from "theater seating," which cramped conversation because everyone had to twist sideways to see each other's faces. As soon as we brought our favorite seats closer together, we found ourselves enjoying more companionable moments.

What about things you use for other activities that you want to do here? Are they somewhere else in the house? Bring them where they belong. Once I got that table in my old place, I took all my board games out of a dresser drawer in my bedroom and put them out in plain view on a shelf in the living room—much more inviting and, I assure you, much more frequently used after the change.

Fine-tune your living room a little today and do some of those things you enjoy!

———

Be yourself, no matter where you are. No matter how small your living space is, honor your essentials.

Balancing on the Edge of a Cliff

Savings Give You Options

30

> Nobody in life gets exactly what they thought they were
> going to get, but if you work really hard and you're kind,
> amazing things will happen. I'm telling you, amazing
> things will happen. I'm telling you, it's just true.
> —*Conan O'Brien, comedian*

Prepare for challenges and opportunities

Now that you've figured out some things you want, save up to make more of them real. To increase your savings, set up an automatic transfer from your checking to your savings account to take place the day after you get paid. If you haven't done it already, set up direct deposit of your paycheck. Streamline the process of your money going to work for you. If your company has a 401k retirement program, look into whether they match funds; it's the simplest way to give yourself a raise.

Sock away that safety net

Already automatically transferring money to savings or retirement funds every paycheck? Good. It's time to take a look and see how you can do more. Canceling memberships you don't use, or changing to less expensive service plans on those you do, can free up some cash. Apply it first to high-interest debt or, if you've conquered that (go, you!), then increase the amount heading into retirement savings. Don't count on social security alone; economic turbulence and lengthening lifespans could upset some of the best-laid plans, so put your nest eggs in more than one basket.

Even if you're living paycheck to paycheck find a way to pull out $10 every check and automatically put it into savings. Figure out the things that would save you the most money (perhaps moving to a new apartment closer to work) or that would help increase your cash flow (maybe a good outfit for interviews and some nicely printed resumes), and do that as soon as these special savings allow.

A good way to begin is to create two savings accounts and autodeposit at least $10–25 per month into each. Use one to build up a general safety net with three months' expenses, and the other as a project fund from which you regularly pull cash when you reach enough for your current special savings goal. Just start them. Increase the monthly deposits as you can, but always put aside at least a dollar or so a day to avoid crisis and improve the tools that you use the most.

Know where your money is going. Are you going deeper into debt or are you paying it off? How have you set up your tax withholding? If you had to pay a huge amount at tax time and your income hasn't changed much, maybe you should increase the withholding to spare yourself the scramble for the money. Did you get a huge tax refund? How about lowering that withholding and setting up an automatic transfer of that cash difference into a retirement account? You won't feel the change throughout the year and your money will be earning you interest instead of the government.

Balance your checkbook and credit card statements every month. This practice will keep you aware of any trends in the flow of your money, as well as giving you the ability to catch bank errors or identity theft while there's time to do something about it.

My financial security rule of thumb: If you are carrying debt with over 6% interest, you should stop using your charge cards and cut optional expenses to the point where you can make significant payments on it every month. Try paying one-tenth of the current balance owed this month if you can, and keep paying at least that dollar amount each month thereafter. That will rid you of that debt within a year.

Bring in more money and spend less

As with so many things, the key to improvement is to change the inflows and outflows.

Work toward getting a raise. (For help with this, see the examples under the agile self development solution in "Symptom #8: The Giant Plan for the Rest of My Life" in Part One.) Make sure you're getting the most matching funds from your employer toward retirement.

Cut expenses for things that don't reward you. Sell the three most valuable things that you don't want to own anymore on eBay or craigslist, or go to an appraiser, have a yard sale, or whatever works best. Turn them into money, take 10–20% of it for something fun, like dinner out, and use the rest to discard some debt.

Enjoy more free stuff. Visit the library. Take advantage of the great entertainment resources online, such as the Internet Archive's OpenLibrary and free songs offered by bands on their websites.

If you do spend money on something, pay less for it. About to go shopping? Think about whether all of it really needs to be brand new. Sure, you don't want hand-me-down underwear or food, but what about a winter coat? A dining table? A bread maker? Get familiar with your local resources. What kind of things do the different thrift stores have? Are you in a craigslist area? Does your community have something like a "pay-and-take" where you can exchange unwanted goods? Don't forget to ask your friends and family. Maybe someone has exactly what you need languishing in a closet and will give it to you, sell it cheap, or swap it for something else.

What's the most beautiful, useful, satisfying second-hand thing you've bought recently? Give yourself credit for saving money and saving energy by reusing. Comparison-shop between new furniture and antiques. My Ikea office cabinet and beautiful 1920s armoire weren't very different in price, but the latter gets much more active use in its place of honor in the living room.

We are in the midst of a cultural shift from consumerism back to collaborative consumption with services like car sharing and projects like NeighborGoods.net blossoming all around the country. Whatever you choose, remember that you have a lot of options beyond what is advertised.

Scratch the going-out itch in a less expensive way. Want to visit that pricy restaurant, but it's outside your budget? Don't go for a full meal.

Have a serving at home of something decent and cheap and then go out for just appetizers at the posh spot. Here's a sneaky tip: You can enjoy them at the bar in many places and avoid the wait for a table.

Vacations often come with lots of hassles, especially if there's an airport involved. Why not save that money, stay at home (or close to it), and spend it on fun stuff? Get a massage, go to a movie, buy 20 new-to-you albums at the used record store. Plan a getaway soon that involves as little driving as possible. Let go of your normal routine and obligations and putter around your favorite neighborhood. I find that the restorative effect is magnified tremendously by doing this on a day you'd normally be at work. Just turn off your mobile phone or leave it at home, so none of those silly people working can distract you from your vacation.

Any time you're at home, take advantage of the opportunity to hunt for buried treasure in your own place. Pull out those old board games, which you haven't played in a long time, and have a Battle of the Games to decide which ones stay and which ones go to charity. Reread old books. Watch old movies again. Extract some of the remaining pleasure from these already invested possessions. When something runs dry, send it on to a new home. You'll be pleasantly surprised to discover how much you have that still can give you a free evening of fun.

Your rich life may not require riches

Saving up for a better life does not need to be an ever-upward climb. Simply figure out what really makes you most happy and relaxed, and continually reposition your world a little closer to getting more of that.

For most people, it isn't yachts and diamonds. It may be as simple as having a job they like, living in a place that they love, and spending time with people whom they enjoy. That's not as expensive as you might think, so take another little step closer to it today. Do what you actually enjoy and strive for your own dreams, not what someone else—especially not some advertiser—tells you that you should want.

31

The Short Leash

You're the Expert on You

> Nothing but human beings here. We try our best,
> we screw up, we act heroically, we take a nap.
> —*Jon Carroll, columnist*

Listen to your wise side

Are you keeping yourself reined in, trying to meet someone else's standard of what is appropriate for you? Stop worrying that you aren't allowed to be gentle or strong or silly or beautiful or whatever you've been telling yourself isn't allowed for people like you.

You're the expert on you. Sure, you can get good ideas and interesting advice all over the place, but no one knows what you need better than you do. Listen. Make time regularly to get back in touch with what you need and want. Take care of yourself as you take care of other demands on your time and energy. Be kind. Be honest. Be brave—most of all with yourself.

Trust that you have learned valuable things. To reconnect with that trust, try writing a letter from "you" now to "you" that you used to be. What would you say to cheer, warn, and teach the person you used to be? Next, imagine receiving a letter from an older and wiser you. What might it say? If you need to hear, "It gets better" (and most of us always do about at least one thing in our lives), what might the path to that happier you look like?

Author and international advisor on education in the arts Sir Ken Robinson gave a very inspiring talk as part of the TED (Technology Entertainment Design) conference. In this lecture—"Bring on the

Learning Revolution!"—in addition to calling for an end to many old, authoritative answers, he reminds us that, "Human communities depend upon a diversity of talent, not a singular conception of ability."

What authoritative answer of what is best for you has, in fact, turned out *not* to fit you? Do not conform to generic expert judgment; instead, fine-tune this wisdom for your unique self.

Discard some dignity

Sometimes the thing you most need is a little silliness. Go ahead and do something harmless and goofy. As cartoonist Walt Kelly's Pogo advised, "Don't take life so serious, it ain't nohow permanent."

Go to a costume party and discard your usual self for a night. Put on a mask, apply another persona, and try out a different way of behaving. Remember how to play make-believe. Who knows? You might learn something interesting about yourself in the process.

Bring back the fun!

What silly thing do you love doing that you haven't done for years? Treat yourself to some pointless pleasure. Play pinball. Break out the coloring books, jacks, or *Candyland*.

Some of us like to relax with games on the computer or video gaming systems. Unless you're blessed with as much free time as you want, and don't have anything else on your list that you'd rather accomplish, you might want to limit the amount of time you spend distracted in these alternate worlds.

When you do play, D. Keith Robinson has a simple suggestion: Play on an easier setting than you normally do. Okay. Maybe you won't be challenging yourself properly, but, really, what's your goal here? To become better at this particular game or relax and have fun? Weigh the satisfaction you achieve after 30 minutes at easy versus hard and go for that which leaves you the jolliest. It's just like tossing a ball around in the yard instead of suiting up for a regulation football game. Who cares if you aren't playing it the tough way? Don't you get enough "tough" elsewhere in your life?

Go have some dumb fun. (You know, happy dumb, not Darwin Awards dumb.) Take a break with a silly movie you love, watch cartoons, tell knock-knock jokes with little kids, or go drinking with a big gang of friends dressed in Santa outfits. Decorate cupcakes. Drive up to the outlook and neck in the backseat. Paint your toenails. Go bowling. Tiaras usually help. (If you really want to get wild, invent a new holiday.)

Loosen up and let yourself be you. Start as small as you need to, but keep tuning in to that inner voice that says, "The real me wants out." It's the 21st century, folks; we can let go of single-context identity. From automobiles, to civil rights, to airplanes, to the Internet, these amazing innovations mean that, since we now can be anywhere doing anything with anybody, we each become, within our individuality, a multiplicity. We're each too big to pigeonhole anymore. Embrace your own diversity.

32

Emotional Baggage

Opt out of Unnecessary Drama

> A man is rich in proportion to
> the things he can afford to let alone.
> —*Henry David Thoreau, philosopher*

Calm helps you cope

There is a moment of choice in how you react which deeply impacts your future self. When facing that moment, "Don't Freak Out" is always the best option.

Maybe you're having one of those postwork evenings that are part restoration and part collapse, and you're watching a movie. The DVD player in your computer jams and the computer won't eject the DVD. Then the computer doesn't believe it has a DVD drive, even after restarting.

You start to work yourself up into an "Oh, no! I can't afford this problem" worried state of mind. Stop and shut down, which helps sometimes with computers, turn the laptop upside down (the disk floats on a spindle), and go take a nice bath. Read a relaxing book (one of Richard Carlson's *Don't Sweat the Small Stuff* series would be ideal).

When you are sufficiently soaked, come out for a brief but unworried test. Turn the laptop over, start it up, hold down the eject button, and out should come the disk, sweet as you please. It doesn't always work that way, although it did for me. Even if it doesn't come out, you'll have had time to remind yourself of people you know who could help you figure out how to fix it, and you'll still have had relaxation time, which was the goal in the first place. Your new mantra can be the phrase attributed to NASA astronaut Fred Haise: "Never panic too early."

Prioritize your energy

Emotional turmoil can almost always move to the bottom of your list. Unless you're overdue for a good cry, or want to punch a pillow, or otherwise blow off a bad steam buildup, there are always more productive things for you to do. Find a little breathing space and give some to others when you can see that they need it. Ease the tension and let something other than drama take your time.

Even the very best group of family or friends can sometimes be annoying, so I encourage you to do two things when stress starts to kick in at big gatherings. When you need a little room, find a way to take it. Good techniques include walking the dog, washing some dishes, amusing the littlest kids, showing the newest family member around the neighborhood, running a last-minute errand, or having a shower. Along with taking care of yourself, make space for others. Build some alone time into your events. Don't make a fuss over people retreating from time to time. Whether between family, friends, or lovers, making room for each other's "me-time" builds stronger relationships

Rescue the stressed. Useful phrases include, "I need a little walk before the pie. Care to come along?," "Mom, I'll do that for you, but sit down for just a moment and tell me again about the trip where you got this vase. That was right after you two got married, right?," "Okay, that's got about an hour more to cook and everything else is all ready, so you all can relax or read or whatever and I'll let you know when we get close to dinner time," and "Who else is ready for a nap break?"

The harmonic intersection

When one particular thing is causing tension in your household, have each of the affected people write down a list of as many acceptable solutions as they can. With any luck you'll find the harmonic intersection that will resolve your domestic discord. For example, when you're trying to keep the house tidy and there's something that one of you thinks is often in the wrong place, each make a list of reasonable locations. You may already have someplace in mind that turns out to be fine with you both. Venn diagram optional.

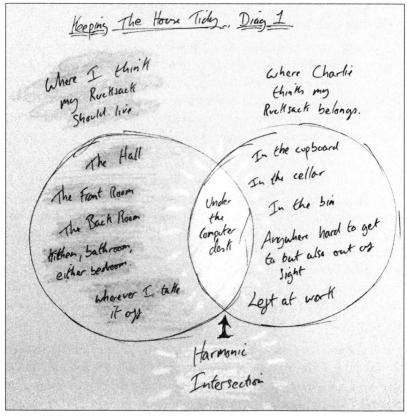

Illustration by Reverend Dan Catt.
(Used by permission. CC by-sa.)

Even when it's a serious disagreement, there are opportunities for peaceful resolution without unnecessary drama. Though parting with someone after eight years together is a painful thing, I have a happy memory of the game an ex and I made of dividing our music CDs. We took turns drawing from the pile, groaning and making notes on our shopping lists and laughing. Even the hard times don't have to be a battle. Letting go of the sadness and anger to find an amicable path is always the right choice.

You are allowed to close the door

What about when you're fighting with yourself? Much of the time, my advice is to "just do it"—push on through your resistance and get that to-do off your list—but, occasionally, that isn't the right answer.

At my old apartment, I had a guest room, which was at one point a halfway house for yard-sale items, unfinished projects, and other miscellanea in a semiconfused state of existence in my daily life. I wanted to clear out the unimportant or no-longer-me stuff and turn it into a space that I would really use. It weighed on me that I was paying rent for that room and didn't make proper use of it.

One day, I had to concede that now was not the time. I had a massively busy schedule at work for the next month. I would be in a state of intense activity every day and had three conferences for which to prepare materials. For the next month, I closed the door. Why was I paying that rent? For the ability to put my personal chaos in another room and not have it detract from the peaceful, soothing nature of the rest of my home.

When you need some clarity and extra calm, find those resources you already have to help accommodate and relieve the stress-causing things in your life. Split the to-do list into must-happen-now and can-wait-until-things-settle-down, and absolutely do not worry about that second list. What was the first thing on my important list? "Stay well and happy and unstressed." What was second? "Support my family and friends as best as I can." What was third? "Perform well at work." What was not on the list? "Clean out the armoire in the guest room."

Make sure that getting organized and uncluttered doesn't leave you overwhelmed all the time. Sometimes the best tactic is to shove that crap in the closet and deal with it later. (Just don't put the bills in there or postpone "later" for too long!)

Work from a foundation of strength

Time out can dilute drama. So, too, can repositioning. Be more grounded with heavy stuff. Move big, hard things closer to your foundation physically and mentally to avoid back pain, earthquake injuries, and unnecessary emotional drama. Handle what's tough from a stronger place. Have intense conversations when you're well rested and can take time to work patiently through the issues. Tackle emotionally loaded discarding when you're feeling good about yourself and well supported by others. Find your firm footing and then take on that challenge you've been avoiding.

Over time, use your moments of peak confidence to strengthen your foundation and eliminate causes of unpleasantness. How can you make your life richer? What expenses of time and energy could you cut out? When you're not sure where to start, look for any big cluster of negative emotions and you'll find something very worthy of letting go.

As Erin Doland said, "If it makes your stomach churn when you see it, this is a pretty good sign that it's time for the item to go."

———

Spend less of your time bathing in emotions that exhaust you.

SIGH

33

Transform that Annoyance

> If it doesn't make sense, challenge it. If it appears
> broken, fix it. If it doesn't work for you, change it.
> —*Michael Lopp*

Lean on that which can be changed for the better

I bet you have a tool you use every week—maybe every day—that bugs you. It's adequate, which is why you haven't replaced it, but it is suboptimal and it slows down your day or doesn't put you in a good mood.

Replace this tool with a better version and learn what a difference truly well-designed things can make. Maybe this means having to do without something else for a little while, but as you skip that fancy coffee drink or pack a lunch or don't go out to dinner, think of all the days ahead where you won't have to put up with that leaky-spouted teapot, low-suction vacuum cleaner, nose-slipping eyeglasses, or streak-leaving windshield wiper blade anymore. Routinely watching for what is suboptimal is an act of optimism. *Really!*

Something around the house bugging you? Is some minor breakage or missing piece holding you back from doing a particular thing or using favorite stuff? Just take care of it. Sew that button back on. Replace that broken drawer pull. Save up and buy a backpack that doesn't have a broken zipper. Change the damn lightbulb already! It'll take less than half an hour and will finally quit annoying you.

There is probably a sharp edge in your life. It's gonna get ya if you don't deal with it. What about that nail starting to come up out of the floor, or toenails that run the risk of hamstringing your spouse one night in bed, or the stupid, decorative, metal light switch cover at the top of the stairs, which threatens to tear a sleeve one of these days? Today, right now, get rid of that problem. Homes shouldn't bite.

Renters: Call your landlord and report broken stuff that they're supposed to fix. Owners: Bring in a pro and take care of the most irritating home flaw. Everyone deserves to live without dripping faucets, broken doorbells, dead stove burners, holes in walls, and similar nonsense.

Make a little quiet time today to look at every room in your house and find the things that aren't how you want them. Particularly watch for two aspects: "easy to change" and "drives me nuts." Fix at least one of the easy ones today, and put in a solid 30 minutes—and remember that writing down a plan can count as progress—on the most crazy-making thing. Shift your world toward "less irritating."

Friday Night Look-Back

One opportunity to identify these annoyances is when you are taking a Friday Night Look-Back. Ask yourself, "What worked well this week?" and optimize for more of this in the future. Also ask, "What wasn't so great?" and upgrade that or phase it out.

> The items you use all the time—your daily tools—will provide the most reward for upgrading them.

Bruce Sterling said, "The everyday object is the monarch of all objects. It's in your time most, it's in your space most. ... the things that you use every day should be the best-designed things you can get." He suggested putting the highest priority on anything placed next to your skin for long periods of time.

Upgrade the source of your aches and pains

One of the best and most simple pleasures, which can really make a difference in your day, is how well you slept the night before. Cut corners on other things so you can have a better bed. A good mattress is a truly wise investment; however, regardless of the type of mattress you have, spend enough time with it.

> Get to bed at a reasonable hour, get a good night's rest, stretch when you get up in the morning, and face the world with a bit more (bed)spring in your step.

If you have a pair of cruel shoes, which leave your feet aching every time you wear them or, worse yet, damage them with blisters and contortions, get rid of those evil bastards! There are sexy shoes that don't cause agony. Another pair out there can make you just as happy as those worn-out ones, which can no longer live up to their former glory (or arch support), once did. Take care of your feet; they work hard for you. As my grandfather and other older friends and relations have warned, healthy feet are an increasingly valuable asset as you get older.

Is there a whole class of clothing that you detest wearing, but that you find hard to avoid? Find an alternative. For me, it's pantyhose. They don't breathe, the tan color looks weird to me, and I hate *hate* **hate** the way the waistband slips down. For years I didn't like wearing dresses or skirts to business or formal events because of the expectation of having to endure pantyhose. Now, when I decide to give up my slacks for something a little more girly, I wear stockings or stocking-top hose in colors and patterns.

What about you? Don't ever want to buy another cotton dress shirt again that isn't wrinkle free? Madam, do you want to replace that bra with a vest top, which includes hidden support? Sir, give yourself permission to grow that beard. "Happy" is a bigger part of "being nice to be with" than "clean-shaven."

Handle efficiently that which you hate

I have to confess something. Unlike many people, I generally hate clothes shopping. The number of choices is overwhelming and the culture, which idolizes disposable fashion and stick-figure thinness, is depressing.

If you also feel this way, here's a tip that made a real difference for me: Figure out a handful of colors that you really like to wear and look good on you. They don't all have to go together, but they should cluster in a couple overlapping groups so you can make the best use of your wardrobe. Poke around in your closets and drawers and note the colors of your favorite clothes.

Think about outfits you like that seem to match up well. If you are colorblind, like lots of folks, have a noncolorblind friend with good fashion sense help you with this. Also, get one of the great smartphone apps, like DanKam: Colorblind Fix to help you day to day. List your colors, decide on half a dozen on which you're going to focus, and figure out the ones that can be worn together.

When you're shopping, look for your colors first. It makes it easy to scan a rack (or a catalog) and zero in on just a few things that might suit you. Then, you can quickly flip through and eliminate things that you don't like about the fabric or details ("too synthetic and shiny," "too busy a pattern," or "too many fiddly lacy bits around the cuffs").

When some things connect, and they're in your price range, try them on to find which one for this manufacturer is flattering to you. Don't let size numbers stress you out; in women's clothing especially, sizes vary radically from brand to brand. Wear what fits your body well.

As you do the "turn the hanger around backwards, put it back the normal way after wearing it, and six months later get rid of the still backwards stuff" trick, you'll find that your closet has largely settled into your chosen colors. There may be a few exceptions, such as dresses or suits for special occasions rather than your mix-and-match outfit ingredients. Shopping for clothes may still not be anything close to your favorite activity, but it can be tolerable.

Do you like shopping *too much*? Tune in to the pattern behind your pleasure. Maybe it's just that moment of acquisition or the quick hit of happiness, which is no different than the one our deepest ancestors felt when their fingers curled around a ripe berry half-hidden under a leaf. However, for most people, there's more to it than that.

Gretchen Rubin, in studying pleasure for her book *The Happiness Project*, came up with a good list of the reasons we make purchases. See if any of these match you: "enjoying keeping your home stocked with good things or making life more convenient, providing for other people, mastering something (e.g., the latest tech gadget), possessing an admired object or maintaining a collection, creating opportunities to teach your children or to expand your expertise, living as your peers do or keeping up with fashion or maintaining traditions, distinguishing yourself from your peers or defying fashion or breaking traditions, beautifying yourself, offering and returning hospitality and support, winning and maintaining status and power, expressing your personality, celebrating, or making life more exciting."

Like Gretchen, I rarely feel "cash register happiness" and, like her, tend to feel buyer's remorse (or as she puts it, "shop shock"). Looking at the list above, it's interesting how many of these potential forms of gratification I get from writing and participating online. If too much stuff or too many bills is a feature of your life that you want to change, figure out the pattern behind your pleasure and start filling in other ways to gratify it that don't add to your load.

Opt out of feeling annoyed

What is far more likely to be irritating to someone than clothes? Computers. Fortunately, unlike physical machines, software is easier to adapt. When you catch yourself swearing at your monitor, see if you can identify a pattern or problem to solve. Perhaps you need to find software that is a better fit for the way you think about this task; maybe you only need to adjust a setting to get the behavior in line with your instincts.

This happened to me with iTunes on the Mac. I spend a great deal of my day in the Firefox web browser, and have reached the point where Command-T—the control to open a new tab—means "jump to where I can do the next thing I want to do." In iTunes I was incessantly hitting that command when I wanted to jump to the currently playing song—to rate it differently or add a comment, for example. Unfortunately, that combination of keystrokes would launch a lovely, full-screen Visualizer lightshow in sync with my music, and I would swear first and then have to escape from it.

To my great relief, when I at last took a couple moments to search on-line for "changing iTunes shortcut keys," I found that the shortcut key choices for many programs—not just iTunes—are completely configurable from the System Preferences "Keyboard" pane. *Astonishing!* Now my instinctive action corresponds to my desired result. Once again, grease the slope toward where you want to be so that your easiest, most automatic behavior takes you there instead of hitting a wall.

Got an annoying commute? Upgrade it by carrying music, earphones, reading material, and the means to jot down notes about ideas. (A smartphone, index cards, and a pen will give you all this functionality.) Peppermints or other flavorful scented candy can also reduce the impact of an unpleasant situation. Maybe that sweaty guy fresh from his gym has nowhere else to sit on the train than beside you, but at least you don't have to spend the whole ride smelling him. Your journey will be happier if you don't have any reason to get worked up about something that's less than optimal. Make it so simple to avoid annoyances that you opt out of feeling annoyed.

———

When the excellence or stress reduction is a great return compared to the cost, find a way to make the investment. Get that extra laptop power cord. What minor purchase could make a chore less likely to pile up? Why not make it easier to do? I certainly shouldn't have delayed as long as I did before buying a $10 delicates wash bag that I could simply toss in the machine!

The principle of not letting it get to you through giving yourself better options applies everywhere. Head your irritation off at the pass by doing something easy early. Prevention is a form of upgrade. A stitch in time really does save nine, whether it's giving yourself the right tools or just unconsciously fine-tuning your environment as you move through it. When your bedroom looks nice merely because you happened to have automatically put away one thing that was in the wrong place every time you entered the room today, then you know that you're getting the hang of this.

34

Bad Scene, Man

Avoid Unnecessary Hassles

> It's amazing how much we can all resist a perfectly
> good enough solution (or choice of what we want
> to do) because it seems too simple.
> —*Jeri Dansky*

Scenario planning

We can avoid much of what irritates us with a little advance thinking, such as the great productive pattern of scenario planning. When you are creating or modifying something—a new furniture arrangement, a new aspect of your routine, or a new way that you want to approach particular social situations—design for the expected use as well as for several possible other conditions, in case major variables switch to other settings than what you had predicted. Prepare yourself for comfortably rolling with the changes.

Writer and futurist Stewart Brand, in *How Buildings Learn* (a book that informs about a much broader range of thinking than merely the architectural), discusses this principle: "All buildings are predictions. All predictions are wrong."

I'll tone it down just a hair: All plans are predictions. No predictions are 100% perfect.

By preparing yourself for imperfection and envisioning reasonable responses to the most likely alternate scenarios, you'll reduce your stress and optimize your results.

Here's an example: Over the past few years I kept reading about treadmill desks and thinking "Wow, that might work great for me. I love walking and I work better when a little of my attention can be busy with something (such as listening to music)." I finally reached a point where I was ready to try it. Instead of just making a plan to switch to the first one I discovered, which would be a major investment, I thought about possible alternate scenarios to "Everything goes as I hope and I love it."

Alternative scenario #1: "I don't love it."

Influence on my plan: Find a way to invest less money on the experiment so it's not too painful if it doesn't work out. (I have more time than money. If you're the opposite, ordering the fancy preassembled solution could work for you if you are satisfied with the company's return policy.)

Alternative scenario #2: "I totally love it and want it permanently, but it takes up too much space and disrupts our use of the room which serves as my office and our guestroom and my partner's desk area."

Influence on my plan: Explore ways to rearrange that room to allow for all the functions for which we currently use it instead of assuming that I need to leave my current workspace where it is.

Alternative scenario #3: "I like it, but my body takes a long time to adjust to working while standing."

Influence on my plan: Create "infrastructure" to support taking care of myself physically. Continue using a rest reminder (I use TimeOut on the Mac) to give myself time away from the keyboard and treadmill. Make a nice seating area near enough to my walking desk where I can step off for a few minutes and rest my body while writing on paper or reading a book or doing something else that doesn't require the computer.

Even a short brainstorming sprint on other things likely to happen besides your favorite prediction will allow you to plan better and build solutions, which can accommodate a variety of futures without breaking.

What was the outcome of my planning? It turned out great—thanks to adjustments that I made to my original idea. I built my own setup using an old bookcase, rearranged the room to better accommodate the treadmill, and made it easy to take my laptop elsewhere for seated work when I want. I wish that I kept some statistics so I could tell you the average miles per hour at which I wrote this book!

If you're lucky, thinking through scenarios at work can sometimes uncover new best practices, which will allow you to eliminate or reduce the number of attendees needed at a recurring meeting. Even if you still need to have meetings there are way to make them less of a hassle for everyone involved. In the invitation, include the goal(s) of the session, any necessary brief introduction to the discussion, and an agenda. When people walk in the door, prime them to be effective and succinct. Don't reward the inconsiderate by starting over or backing up unless absolutely necessary; people will learn that you mean business and don't intend to waste their time. If you do this, your meetings will run faster and better.

A timely note to your future self

Some other things besides badly run meetings are a tedious pain in the butt. For instance, you run out of prescription allergy medicine and have to wait in line to renew it, instead of doing it online (or by mail), because you threw away the box with the prescription number. Not having a magic number, which is the key to resolving a problem, can make a chore seem more than twice as big and can delay you for days. You can avoid this kind of situation by planning.

In your contacts on your phone, or in an easily looked-up message to yourself in a web-based email program like Gmail, note numbers that would save you a ton of time to have later: prescription numbers; ink cartridge model number for your printer (or other details you frequently need in order to complete an errand); rental or homeowners insurance account number; the phone number of an out-of-area friend or relation, who could help you in case of a natural disaster; your sizes and measurements, plus those for whom you often buy clothes; membership numbers because, if they're in your phone, you don't have to carry all the dang cards with you all the time; and your landlord and neighbor's phone numbers.

Because of identity theft risks, you shouldn't list your social security number and credit card numbers (though the contact numbers for lost cards are useful). Having this available to you from anywhere, online, can avoid a world of hassle in a crisis. For the same reason, you may also want to put this information on a thumb drive and keep it in your emergency kit.

Back it up

Losing all your computer data is a *really* sucky inconvenience—and you will face that risk sooner or later. As technology journalist and civil liberties activist Danny O'Brien put it, "Power users trust software as far as they have thrown their computers in the past."

No more excuses! Do a backup today and create a plan for regular backups in the future. The most convenient approach is an overall solution for your whole system, such as Time Machine on the Mac. At the least, make copies of important things, such as your writing, your photos, your address book, and the one file that would most make you cry if lost.

Store the copies away from your home, either online or otherwise. Remember that in addition to physical media under your control (external drives, CDs, DVDs, second computers), you may also have some space for things on a hosted service. For example, if you own your own domain and have hard drive space on a server as part of the hosting of your website, you could store some backup files there, carefully putting them in a nonpublic folder. Remember, though, that if that service goes out of business, the backup could be lost to you and, if it gets hacked, personal data could be stolen. Be selective about how you use these resources. It's advisable to make a big backup periodically and store it in two separate locations away from your home (e.g., in an online service and on DVDs that you keep at work).

Regularly—every week or at least every month is advisable and I strongly urge you to automate this so it will happen far more often, even multiple times a day—make a backup of those things that have changed since the last backup. When you do this backup, I recommend keeping the previous two backups. That way, should you lose your current information and turn out to have a damaged backup, you still have the prior ones.

In the absence of a good automated solution like Time Machine, doing backups can be tedious and is easy to put off, so figure out a good system that works for you and make sure you have the supplies you need. Get help from a geek friend if you're not sure of the process or the best approach for you. Build time into your schedule to do backups regularly and confirm that your system is working correctly with backups that are actually good. It may seem like a hassle but, compared to the loss of all your personal files, it's not a big deal at all.

Don't leave the keys in the lock

While you're roaming around the online world, use good sense when creating and maintaining your passwords. As every hacked system's list of user passwords reveals, people often fail to take this simple precaution. When Gawker Media was hacked in 2010 the top three passwords, each used by over 1,000 users, were "123456," "password," and "12345678."

Please don't be one of those people who leaves their virtual keys in the lock. Make passwords at least eight characters long, using a mix of numbers and letters, with at least one letter capitalized. Most importantly, don't use the same password for everything; at minimum, make sure the things that you most want to protect (for example, your online banking) don't share a password with other, less well-protected services.

Little changes, big risk protections

Don't increase your risks by living in a state of denial. Joining my community's neighborhood emergency preparedness team has taught me to practice prevention for the big stuff as well as the little. Getting your household ready to ride out trouble turns out not to be that hard. Change the battery in your smoke alarm and test any other warning and safety equipment in your home and car. Have appropriate fire extinguishers in good, charged condition in the kitchen and at least one other place in the house. Have renter or homeowner's insurance and an up-to-date inventory of the things you'd want to replace. Walk around with a video camera for a quick way to do this inventory and then—important!—store the tape away from the house. Do what you can to prevent losing what matters to you.

When it comes to our own safety, it's common to err on the side of "I'll be fine." For that reason, it's good to know the real risks. For example, when a utility pole falls down, assume that the lines are live, charged electrical wires and that the danger zone extends wider than just the immediate area of the downed wire to the second intact pole from the point of impact. If you're wrong and it's not live, no harm done; being mistaken the other direction could be fatal.

Understanding risks helped my old schoolmate, artist Debby Kaspari, and her husband Mike survive an F3 tornado, which passed right through their house. Even though they didn't really feel like a direct hit would ever happen to them, they own and use a weather radio. About a decade ago, they had a steel box shelter installed in the floor of their garage. When the warning came, they had the good sense and the resources to grab the cat and go below to wait out the storm. The house above them was destroyed, but a little preparation and caution allowed them to walk away without a scratch.

Here's a classic question to help reveal your personality: "If your house were on fire, what would you save?" Unfortunately, if you really do try to save things, you dramatically increase your risk of being injured or killed. Discard your illusions about house fires. There is no time in a fire for anything but getting out and calling the fire department from a neighbor's house. Get a smoke alarm and check with your local fire department for more details on how to protect your household from fire and natural disasters. Many places offer free preparedness training, which can save your life as well as lower your stress before, during, and after a catastrophic incident.

Remember: Life is the essential ingredient to quality of life.

——

If you've already decluttered your bathroom, this next step is going to be much easier; however, no matter how easy or hard it is, the payoff for doing it can make an enormous difference when you need it the most.

It's time to get your first aid kit (or kits) organized. The Red Cross and similar organizations have detailed information on their websites about what you need in a general first aid kit and to survive any special threats to which your region is prone. Pull together all your various medical emergency supplies. See what you have already for the kit, and start a shopping list for what you need to add. You don't have to do it all at once, just start.

You may find that you have more than you need of some things, so separate things out and start kits for your office or car. Alternatively, buy a good kit from the Red Cross and, after you get it, donate all the old jumble of stuff to your local shelter except what you'll use to restock your kit for regular home use (e.g., adhesive bandages in your favorite sizes). Think and prepare now, at your leisure, instead of in a rush later when everyone else is scrambling for the same supplies at the stores.

You can't always do it all, and that's okay

Even when you aren't in the midst of a disaster, circumstances can hit you and having some safety nets will make an enormous difference. If something suddenly takes up all your time and energy—medical crisis, new baby, crazy rush at work—it's very helpful to be able to give the sudden event the necessary attention without having it throw other things even more out of balance.

Direct deposit and automatic bill pay can come to your rescue when you need to get through a demanding time and think about nothing at all. Drinking enough water, eating decent meals—especially breakfast—and getting as much sleep as you can will help keep your body supporting the pressure on your mental focus and your emotions. If you have to work through a surprise stressful situation—say, a family member having major surgery—it's very likely that you'll be short on sleep or at least have somewhat disturbed sleep. You'll certainly be working yourself harder mentally and emotionally to bear this extra load along with whatever else is going on in your life.

You're going to be stretched a little thin when it comes to restedness. You may find that—when the initial danger passes, when other people arrive to help take the load, or after a week or so without relief—a lot of tension that you'd been fending off suddenly falls squarely onto you and you become exhausted and emotional. It's completely natural; don't feel badly. Do the minimum you need to do that day and then go home. Eat something nourishing (stop for takeout, if that works), and drink some water or juice, and then go to bed. Never mind if it's before 8pm.

Here's the important part: If tomorrow is a workday, set your alarm clock right now. It may be that you won't fall asleep right away, but that's okay. Don't watch TV. Just feel safe and cozy and maybe read something restful for a bit. If your energy is drained, you'll conk out soon and you may sleep for 10 to 12 hours. If you do, you needed it. Charging your batteries is part of helping get you and the people you love through anything hard. Don't try to get by without doing it.

Clear communication with friends, family, and significant others can reduce the potential for drama, which is usually the last thing you need during hard times. Say something like, "I'm putting all my energy into [whatever is going on] and I'm afraid it's going to make me [spend less time with you, be unfocused, be unusually emotional]. I'm sorry in advance if that turns out to be the case, and I truly do appreciate any slack you can give me while I'm getting through this." It won't solve everything, but it should weed down the number of "Why didn't you come to my party?" whines.

Most of all, be honest with yourself. Prioritize and let stuff go. Do the most important things well and skip or skimp on other things. You can't always do it all and that's okay.

Cushion yourself against the little irritations, too

Help yourself avoid headaches outside of a crisis. Communicate clearly now to save time and avoid hassles later.

> At the start of your day, identify what absolutely must happen today as well as one other thing on which you most want to make progress. Keep focusing on those things until they're done.

Next time you have to travel, think ahead and bring the stuff you run around trying to find and on which you spend too much money. Have a master calendar and add everything that affects more than one person in the household, which keeps everyone coordinated. Even a simple thing like storing the trash bags in the bottom of the bin, so it's effortless to restore the bin to use after you take the trash out, can make your future days more pleasant. Whenever you see an opportunity to take a little time now to save yourself more later when things may be hectic, take advantage of it.

One last and almost entirely avoidable hassle is agonizing over having to wait for someone. Whether it's a long line, a delayed appointment, or a broken-down subway, sometimes you'll be stuck waiting. You know this will happen, so prepare things that will allow you to consider it a treat, like an unexpected downtime bonus or a surprise lull granting you a pleasurable moment. You'll be astonished at how much more tolerable errands and appointments can be if you're prepared.

———

What could you take care of this week that would most dramatically reduce your risk of future hassle? Improve your odds and do it now.

35

Overspending, Underenjoying

Bang for Your Buck

> Avoid a life of chasing prizes not worth winning.
> —*Caterina Fake, entrepreneur*

Contentment doesn't always have a price tag

Above a certain baseline, the correlation between money and happiness grows weak; however, we easily fall into the habit of spending too much and getting too little return on our investment. A financially struggling startup once laid me off, and I went through considerable stress over how I could possibly enjoy life while I got by on unemployment insurance and hunted for a new job.

A wise friend walked with me to a beautiful park in the middle of a warm weekday, and pointed out that I now had access to all kinds of free or cheap pleasures, for which I'd been substituting while putting in my long days at the startup. Don't tie your perception of relaxation or satisfaction to the act of spending money; they aren't the same thing at all.

Drop the unrewarding extras

What do you shell out money for every month? Sure, rent or mortgage, utilities, and food, but what about nonessentials? Look at your routine expenses and the time you spend enjoying their results.

How many hours do you watch those extra cable channels? What are you therefore paying per hour for that service? Do you still want to spend time that way or are there other things you'd do if the temptation weren't there? Do you read the paper every day? Is it worth the subscription? What about the magazines you get or that gym membership? Are there free exercise methods you'd use just as often? Is food spoiling in the fridge before you eat it? It doesn't matter if it's a small expense; if it's not giving you enough benefit, then stop spending that money. Save it or spend it on something that matters to you more.

As you focus on what you want and don't want in your life, there are probably some things for which you'd like to save up some money. It can be hard to do that, though, if you never seem to have extra at the end of the week. Keep your eyes on the prize. Look at what you have to spend each month (for rent, bills, payments to reduce debt, and groceries) and what that leaves you for flexible expenses. Assign yourself an amount that you can spend each week (or fortnight or month) on optional things.

Tape two index cards together on the long edge. On the left, write the list of things for which you want to be saving up and the amount it will take to do so. On the top right, put the amount you have assigned yourself as available for optional things ($100 in the example below). Enter *every* nonessential purchase and deduct it. Before making a nonessential purchase, you'll see your wishlist on the left side and think about whether this purchase is really worth it. You'll also get a clearer picture of where your money goes.

For example, here's what the right side might look like:

$100		
$95	*latte & croissant*	*$5*
$92	*mocha*	*$3*
$82	*new TMBG album*	*$10*
$77	*latte & croissant*	*$5*
$74	*mocha*	*$3*
$54	*pizza & beer night*	*$20*
$49	*latte & croissant*	*$5*

If one of the things on the wishlist side was "espresso machine $200," it's pretty obvious that it won't take that long to save up for it by not going out for coffee drinks (or you could recoup the cost by buying it now). If the other thing on the wishlist is an exercise bike, knocking off the croissants will not only help save up for that but will also make it less necessary.

When you need to conquer debt as well as save up for new expenses, try taking your charge cards out of your wallet and securing them at home. Wait 24 or more hours before making nonessential purchases. Start paying more than the minimum due on the bill and get yourself out of living in a credit crunch. Mediocre mochas may be a bad way to spend your money, but they guarantee more enjoyment than bank finance charges. Knock out the needless expenses first, and then improve your imperfect ones.

Beware of false savings

In my time, I've had memberships to huge warehouse stores. Costco is the archetype for this, but other similar places offer "great deals" when buying in larger quantities. Let's put aside for now the mental stretch of envisioning one's life 20 bars of soap into the future. I find that, after the initial glut of buying many things for relatively less money, I spend more in a warehouse store than I would by shopping at neighborhood stores—even pricier than average ones—and end up with more than I can use or with things that I don't really need.

Even sillier, I wind up buying not quite what I wanted—different brands, other flavors, higher calories—because the selection is more limited. Take a good hard look at your shopping habits and the kind of eating habits to which they're leading. Try taking a month off from the big-box stores.

Remember: Locally owned, independent merchants return significantly more of their money to *your* local economy. Get more fresh fruit and vegetables, pick out ingredients with which to cook, or make a sandwich for tomorrow's lunch instead of a frozen entree. Visit the farmers' market and find the good bakery nearest to your house.

At the end of the month see how you feel, and notice what you're eating and what you've spent. Chances are pretty good that the delicious organic produce, which is giving you loads more energy, has been easily afforded by not having unexpectedly bought a boxed set of DVDs for a show you liked when you were 12, a five-attachment cordless drill you still haven't used, and a pair of ill-fitting orange sneakers with totally cool treads. As a bonus, you may find yourself buying smarter and eating smarter. When you prepare meals from scratch, the food already begins to satisfy your senses before the first bite. Right-size your intake.

Don't overspend your health

Read the can or bottle of the beverages you're drinking today. Here's a good example of the kind of thing some of you might find: carbonated water, caramel color, aspartame, phosphoric acid, potassium benzoate, natural flavors, citric acid, and caffeine.

What do those ingredients do to your body? Are you draining yourself or fueling yourself? Drink more water and start cutting out the sugary (or fake sugary) caffeine bombs. If you're relying on the bump from your drinks to get you through the day, you're masking a bigger problem and making your body pay the price.

Enjoy what you've got

Maybe tonight's a good night to stay home, make some dinner from ingredients you already have or heat up some leftovers, watch the movie that's been sitting around, read a book off that stack in the corner, or play a favorite old game that's been gathering dust. Without spending, you can have a really nice time and remind yourself what is good about your life. Consider how you can increase your opportunities to lounge on porches and by crackling fireplaces. Experiences are often a better investment than objects.

———

When you do spend, target it toward what brings you the greatest returns. What gives you pleasure disproportionate to its cost? Enjoy that more often. Hate cleaning but love to cook? Hire a maid service, enjoy the freedom from some chores that you hate, and offset the cost by eating out less and making more great meals in your nice clean kitchen.

Love city life, especially dining out, but hate your long commutes from the suburbs? Move to a little apartment or condo in a great neighborhood nearer to work and ditch the car. You can make much more enjoyable use of the hundreds of dollars you've been spending on gas, car payments, insurance, maintenance, parking, and tickets.

With a magic wand, what would you eliminate from your life (e.g., housework or driving in traffic) and what would you add (e.g., culinary adventures or convenient nightlife)? Don't assume that it's impossible. Start brainstorming about all the ways you can trade the bad for the good.

Boredom, Lethargy, Apathy

Set Aside Your Short Attention Span

36

> I don't know what people do who don't do anything!
> — *Mary Sanders, my grandmother*

Set yourself free from self-inflicted traps

Are you bored and lethargic? Sometimes it's a retreat from stress elsewhere in your life; sometimes it's frustration causing you to give up and be a lump. Boredom is definitely a trap you build yourself, and it can be the easiest to escape.

The cure for boredom is to stop doing that kind of "doing nothing" where your mind isn't still. Turn off the TV. Cover it up and pretend that you don't have one. Don't turn on the computer if your form of ennui involves mindless surfing and evenings lost to unsatisfying chats. Make something. Write a letter (you know, on paper!). Spend time with someone old and ask them to tell you about their favorite things to do when they were in their teens. Learn to cook. Reconnect with one longtime friend every day for a week. Keep yourself from wasting time in the unfulfilling ways that have become a habit and remember that you have good options.

Stretch your mind

Discard the illusion that you can't keep yourself amused with just your mind. If you're out of practice, start building your wool-gathering muscle. Slow down and think. Build dreams. Follow a complex trail of ideas through its twists and turns. Examine your assumptions. Imagine alternatives.

Set aside your short attention span

Sometimes a thing takes longer. Sometimes you need to mull it over for a while. What have you been giving less attention than it deserves? Stop rushing around; slow down and focus. If the goal in your life is not to have read as many blog posts and flipped through as many magazines and watched as many shows as time and caffeine allow—and I certainly hope it is not—then what do you want to have done with yourself? On what would you like to be looking back at the end of this year? Go do some of that.

As author Annie Dillard said, "How we spend our days is, of course, how we spend our lives."

Re-examine your real bottom line

Have you been living as though the acquisition of stuff was your primary goal? If so, what kind of life is that approach giving you? Most of the rest of the world gets by on less than you can imagine.

Thanks to a lucky business trip I had the opportunity to visit Africa. I loved it and learned valuable lessons I still carry with me. After I visited the home of a woman named Miriam in an informal settlement in Soweto, and chatted with her as she cooked on a paraffin stove in her two-room, jury-rigged shack, the quantity of stuff in my apartment alarmed me.

Miriam didn't have many things, but everything in her possession had a purpose. Her home was painfully simple—and I hope that she realized her dream of moving into a more solid home with indoor plumbing—but she had put her heart into it and made it clean and cheerful.

She crafted her wallpaper from bright green wrappers from a household product and painted the exterior brightly. She swept the dirt floor scrupulously and a few plants were growing in her yard. After visiting Miriam's house, a girl's orphanage near Nairobi, and a Maasai village, it was very clear to me that it is not the number or newness of possessions that make a happy home.

Compared to most of the rest of the world, we're rich. I realized how much I'd taken for granted the luxury of a solid, nonleaky house; indoor toilets; a fuel supply and plentiful clean water piped right into the house; a great variety of fresh foods; and clean clothes in good condition. As we begin to appreciate more of what we have, and buy fewer new things and get rid of things we don't need, it makes it easier to afford (or notice that we could already afford) to contribute to other people's quality of life.

Sometimes that bit of money comes from skipping something that we realize isn't really worth it. At other times, it comes from acknowledging that something brings us enough pleasure and is worth an investment for the long term. Once we do the math we may figure out that ad hoc purchases are actually costing us a lot more than we really need to spend. What are your true minimums? Think about where your money goes versus where you want it to be going.

Make that sweet little connection

When the news is dark or you're facing setbacks, remember the good advice of my friend, spiritual entertainer John Halcyon Styn: "Sometimes you need to turn off the news and focus on the faces in your real life. Sometimes you need to focus on even the smallest of steps that you can make, personally, toward love and compassion."

The next time you're feeling disinterested in everything, make some effort to reconnect. Start by connecting to yourself, and the rest of the world will get easier. Clean up your desk or project space, and then spend an hour doing the most creative thing you do there—writing, sewing, drawing, whatever you like. Clear the dining room table and the kitchen counters of stuff that doesn't belong there. Wash the dishes so the sink is ready for action, and then plan a nice meal. Head out to the farmers' market, if you have one in your area today, to shop for ingredients. Take care of your body and get that massage, haircut, manicure, or whatever you've been putting off.

There's no sin in "sincere," even—perhaps especially—when it's got a touch of silliness. Go ahead. Start a show on the web and convince enough people around the world to lay pieces of bread on the ground to make an Earth sandwich (like humorist and artist Ze Frank). Make videos that show how every sound in them comes into being (like the band Pomplamoose's Nataly Dawn Knutsen and Jack Conte). Write songs from the point of view of a giant squid or Pluto's moon Charon (like musician Jonathan Coulton). Decide that a bar on a Saturday night is the perfect venue for literary readings and launch an absurdly fun series that will last over a decade (like author and commentator Charlie Jane Anders).

Instead of being bored, create something good—a happier home, a healthier you, a creative work of art, a great relationship, a beautiful tool, a positive vision of what your life could be like, or a random act of kindness. Take a step toward better. *Just one step.* It's more rewarding, enjoyable, and full of potential than wallowing in a lethargic mental swamp.

37

The Edison Museum

Moore's Law

> Obsolescence never meant the end of anything—
> it's just the beginning.
> —*Marshall McLuhan, educator and philosopher*

Format is not the same as function

While you're upgrading your life, give your media an upgrade as well. It can be all too easy to hold onto the physical carriers for our media experiences long past our desire to engage with that content in that format again. Even if you strongly associate an album or film with a period of growth that helped make you who you are today, keeping this old copy is not what maintains the influence it had on you.

Audio/visual day

Take a paper sack and go to where you keep all your videos and DVDs. Find the ones you don't plan to watch again in the next year and put them in the sack. We will sort through the sack later, so go ahead and put in those old family videos. Hunt down the other stashes of video entertainment and do the same. Got a box of old 8mm home movies in the basement? Bring it up. Find every form of generating a flickering image on a screen and pull together all the examples that you have to confess you won't watch this year.

Sort these media items into three groups:

1. Ones to return it to their rightful owners;

2. Anything that wasn't mass produced (e.g., those old family films) or with which you're determinedly not ready to part, despite not watching it every year; and

3. Everything else.

Put all the #1 items with other things to return to the library or to individuals. Sort the #2 items by media.; they are now archiving or replacement projects. DVDs are probably okay for the moment but, since it's easy, I'd recommend making a backup copy of anything home produced that could not be replaced. Movies on laser discs are almost certainly replaceable with current media. Do you still use the laser disc player? Don't keep things you don't have now or plan to get soon a means on which to play it.

Videos are kind of a pain. If you still have a video cassette recorder, which works great and which you use regularly, then it's probably fine to have a box of old home videos in the basement. However, I strongly recommend periodically backing up home-produced items onto alternate media, such as DVDs since all magnetic materials degrade and you might as well move things to a format that's more convenient to turn into multiple copies.

For videos and older movie formats, such as film, it's advisable to read up on how to store them for optimal survival and to investigate ways to make backup copies on current formats. Most communities have services that will transfer old media to new. This can be a very good investment for families, who want to have multiple copies of those movies of great-grandpa and grandma.

Donate all the #3 things to charity.

In short, keep the things you use, protect the things you don't use regularly but treasure, and get the other stuff out of your way.

Tune tune-up

Repeat this process with your music, whether digitally stored or in physical form. Over time, your opinions and tastes change. Look around your place. Do you have a collection in pride of place that you actually never play? If you've made the switch to digital storage, does your home know that?

My friend, author and community consultant Derek Powazek, describes his moment of recognition: "My CDs had become this snapshot of who I was, like carrying around a driver's license with a 5 year-old photo where you're wearing old glasses and a shirt you wouldn't be caught dead in now. And here I was displaying them like a shrine in an immense tower in my living room."

Go through your physical music media—CDs, records, mini-discs, cassettes, 8-tracks, reel-to-reel tapes, wax cylinders, or whatever you've got your tunes on—and gather all the things you don't care that much for anymore. Sell them, trade them online through a site like Swap.com, or give them away.

Delete all the music on your computer and any other music player that makes you say, "Meh." There is better stuff out there for you. If you're like me, you're using your CDs as a storage device and listening to your music in MP3 form, often in shuffle play or playlists. If you're like me, you've also learned over time that there are songs on albums that just don't do it for you. So why would you want that stuff to come up in shuffle play? Why should it take up your hard drive space?

My friend, artist B.J. West, observed, "It really is amazing how thinning an artist you have *waaaay* too much of makes shuffle so much more pleasant."

Optimize for music you truly like. I use iTunes ratings to mark things with two stars that might be destined for removal when they just ain't it and I can't think of the last time when I was in the mood when they would be right. The second time they disappoint, I set them down to one star; the third time, they hit the digital trash, and I remove them from iTunes and my hard drive. Periodically I compare my albums in iTunes with my physical CDs, which are stored in a closet, and get rid of anything that's no longer represented on my computer.

"At some point in life, removing music from iTunes becomes as satisfying as adding music used to be," said humorist James Lileks.

Fine-tune for satisfaction.

———

Now that you've cleared things out, bring in new good stuff! Find new films and music to stretch your brain. Go to festivals. Listen to local bands. Check out music-recommending services like Pandora, Last.fm, and Spotify. Ask your friends to bring something over for a movie night or make a mix of music they think you'll like. Open yourself up to new opportunities and take advantage of the flexibility of the digital age.

38

But I Spent a Lot On It!

Keeping and Not Using Does Not Generate Value

> Chronic remorse, as all the moralists are agreed, is
> a most undesirable sentiment. If you have behaved
> badly, repent, make what amends you can and address
> yourself to the task of behaving better next time. On
> no account brood over your wrong-doing. Rolling in
> the muck is not the best way of getting clean.
> —*Aldous Huxley, author*

Avoiding the guilt of bad buying decisions

Why do we allow ourselves to spend on transitory experiences, such as food and movies, but then get ourselves in twist over spending on objects? We often wrestle with the insidious feeling that, if we get rid of this object, it will mean we wasted our money. When this happens, it causes us to behave as if somehow, by keeping the object around, we are improving our chances of compensation for the expense. *We aren't.*

Think longer about purchases before making them. Recognize that you will make some bad decisions. As Discardian Janet Katz of Austin, Texas, put it, "Did you get your money's worth? If you are ditching a $5 paperback book, did you enjoy it $5 worth? If you did, then, like a loaf of bread you ate, you got your money's worth."

It's not odd to support a restaurant by buying a meal you're merely going to eat or to support a band by going to see a show that will be over in a couple hours, so why not support an author by buying a book you plan to read and then sell or give away?

Once you've gained what you needed to get or learn from something—including an emotion—it's perfectly acceptable and often helpful to let it go.

Just because you've gotten what you needed out of something, it doesn't mean that it can't still do some good in the world. See if a charity will accept it. Computers, cellphones, eyeglasses, appliances, and cars are all costly things that can have a useful life beyond your time with them. A few minutes of online research can lead to relief from guilt and a less cluttered house!

Enjoy your good stuff

The flipside to this coin is the stuff you fail to enjoy because you spent so much on it but which you know would still bring you pleasure.

My friend, writer and mom Meg Hourihan, spoke poignantly of this dilemma: "I'd keep bottles of wine and treasure jars of jam for so long they'd be no good once I got around to using them. I decided life was too short and that it was important to use the good stuff. And now I do, mostly. I saved a beautiful birthday gift of 1989 Laurent-Perrier Champagne too long (no situation ever seemed good enough to justify its drinking) and when I opened it, it was passed and I was so sad. It was just the kick in the pants I needed to remember to use the good stuff."

Journalists and wine critics Dorothy J. Gaiter and John Brecher of *The Wall Street Journal* recommend that you quit waiting for some occasion special enough for that most special bottle onto which you've been holding for years: "We invented Open That Bottle Night [OTBN] for a simple reason: All of us, no matter how big or small our wine collections, have that single bottle of wine we simply can never bear to open. Maybe it's from Grandpa's cellar or a trip to Italy or a wedding. We're always going to open it on a special occasion, but no occasion is ever special enough. So it sits. And sits. Then, at some point, we decide we should have opened it years ago and now it's bad anyway, so there's no reason to open it, which gives us an excuse to hang onto it for a few more decades. So OTBN—which is now always the last Saturday in February—offers a great opportunity to prepare a special meal, open the bottle and savor the memories."

If you have to, you can wait until February, but wouldn't tonight be good enough for a special meal with those closest to you and a toast to the past and the future over a glass of something fine?

When it comes to the good stuff, you deserve to be enjoying even the nonperishables sooner. It's actually better for the world if you upgrade even the long-lasting things. Well-made things are more sustainable than cheap ones.

As Bruce Sterling put it: "Stuff breaks, ages, rusts, wears out, decays. Entropy is an inherent property of time and space. Understand this fact. Expect this. The laws of physics are all right, they should not provoke anguished spasms of denial. ... Get excellent tools and appliances. Not a hundred bad, cheap, easy ones. Get the genuinely good ones. Work at it. Pay some attention here, do not neglect the issue by imagining yourself to be serenely 'non-materialistic.' There is nothing more 'materialistic' than doing the same household job five times because your tools suck."

"Better for the world" and "nicer to you" is a great combination. Cult of Less creator and engineer Kelly Sutton has seen a big benefit to his very minimalist approach: "Now every purchase I make comes with a second-guess: Do I really need this? Like really, really need this? In the past year, 'impulse buy' has left my vocabulary. I found myself buying fewer things, but also nicer things. ... Every possession also requires a certain amount of upkeep, and I find myself with more time and less possessional guilt."

Let the bad choices go and give yourself just the things you'll constantly use with pleasure.

39

Killing Time

Living in the Present

I know you all have ideas sitting in the back of your
head; go out and start it. I mean, there's no reason not to.
Don't be afraid.
—*Will Smidlein, teen entrepreneur*

Don't live the life of having to make the time pass

Don't spend your time hanging on for tomorrow, clockwatching, and
merely enduring. Do what you love whenever you can. Laugh long and
hard at anyone who says you're done living and that it's time to buckle
down to "real life," by which they mean horrible dullness.

There is absolutely no excuse for failing to notice repeatedly that
existence is bloody brilliant! Fantastic things are going on all the time,
even in the worst of times, if you only watch for them.

Discard passivity!

Don't just consume some corporate product; make things! Support your
fellow creators. I love to go to the Maker Faire festival of do-it-yourself
arts, crafts, and technology to see the range of things that people are
doing because it pleases them to do so. General geekery and personal
passion everywhere you look. What interests you? What gives you deep
enjoyment? Look around tonight and think about those projects you
started but never finished or always wanted to do.

Instead of turning on the TV or otherwise blobbing out after work
this week, fit in some creative time to tinker. Give yourself space—physical, mental and chronological—to play. Life deserves joy, enthusiasm,

and simple pleasures. Go ahead. Make a city out of Legos, make a quilt out of favorite old t-shirts, learn backyard rocketry, or turn an old book cover into a clutch purse—whatever you like. Do something for the pleasure of doing it, and learn how it works. Nothing wrong with being easily pleased; you get to spend more time being pleased.

Home projects don't have to be hard or huge. You can find great ideas on sites like NotMartha.org and useful help on sites like Flickr and WikiHow. Try searching for the topic in which you're interested as "tags." For example, you can find a tutorial on how to make paper that is tagged *howto, papermaking, paper, craft* and *art*. In addition to the *howto* tag, try *tutorial* and *diy* (do it yourself). You can also find tips on how to make a photocomic or, for real beginners, a nice warm-up exercise about how to enjoy Kraft Macaroni & Cheese. Everybody knows how to do something, so get out that camera and add your own tutorials.

———

Corporate-produced entertainment costs money, usually involves advertising, and not infrequently leaves us unsatisfied. Contrast that with the results of creating. "The feeling that I did this myself and it's good, often beats the feeling that Professionals did this for me and it's perfect," observed writer and teacher Clay Shirky.

It's time for a creative burst! Revive dormant arts. Use the next month to stretch, try some new things, make some mistakes, and level up your inventive skills. Write, sing, play instruments, take pictures, make movies—whatever you feel like doing. Share it with a friend or a bunch of friends. There are lots of free ways to share things online, but maybe tonight will be great for participating in a jam session with some pals, having a cup of coffee with a writing buddy, hosting a creative open house to replace happy hour at the bar, or letting your kids cast you in their new theatrical production. Go, do, make!

———

Have you ever tried to create a game? It's fun! Although it can take a bit of rule tweaking to get a good play balance, the more games you try to make, the better you'll get at making them. Break out paper, pencils, crayons, dice, cards, pieces from other games, or anything you think might be good ingredients for your creativity. Think about aspects of games you enjoy and incorporate them. Get your friends and family to help improve it.

Plug your mind into new connections

Do you have fond memories of interesting elective college classes or wish you'd been able to attend college at all? Fill your iPod with lectures from your library's nonfiction CD collection. Go for a walk or to the gym and stretch your body and mind.

Are you getting as much out of your commute as you could? My congratulations if you find it to be valuable and rewarding time. I suspect, though, that many people feel quite the opposite.

When last I had a long commute, I upgraded it by trading driving for walking and transit. I got a refreshing three-block walk down my hill, a short ride on the subway, a two-block walk over to the Transbay bus terminal, and usually a good 15 to 20 minutes of comfortable riding over the Bay Bridge to a stop three blocks from work. By the time I reached the office, I'd woken up properly and seen pretty views from my high seat going over the bridge.

It was valuable because I could download my email before I left the house and sort through it all before I got to the office. I was often able to compose answers for all the quick questions and usually had time left over to plan the rest of my day. When I arrived at the office and plugged in, I sent out my messages and moved on to the appropriate next action, rather than just reacting to whatever was coming at me.

On the way home, I usually relaxed and looked out the windows at the view. Sometimes I read or watched a bit of a DVD on my laptop. (Old TV shows with which I was catching up were particularly suited to this.) I know folks who drive and listen to audiobooks to make their commutes more relaxing and to let them reclaim desired reading time. There are other tricks for the car as well, such as practicing a new language or keeping up with your daily news intake through podcasts or thoughtful radio programs. Look at your routine and see how you might make it serve you better.

Put pen to paper

Put your friend's and family's addresses in something small and easy to carry (e.g., a mobile phone or a teeny address book). Make especially sure that you have the complete addresses of any person who is either under the age of 20 or over the age of 60. If you have old blank postcards around, grab 'em and a couple of pens with which you like to write. Buy more postcards if necessary, or find amusing ones among displays with free advertising, which often turn up in restaurant hallways by the bathrooms. You can also get a bunch of postcard-size pieces of blank paper and draw doodles on them instead of the usual pictures.

Walk down to the post office and buy a packet of postcard stamps. Sit in a nice café or teahouse and write quick notes to everyone, just saying hi. Mail them and make sure that you still have more postcard stamps to carry with you. Next time you see a nice postcard—especially one of those free ones—grab it and take a couple of minutes to brighten someone's day.

Get sweetly messy

If it's raining, bake something—even you noncooks! Go down to the store and get something ready to bake, like biscuits or cinnamon rolls or cookies. Take some to a neighbor and get acquainted. If it's not raining, plant some flowers—a windowbox, a curbside planting area, your garden, or an elderly neighbor's garden. Get some dirt and life into your senses.

———

Whatever you do, choose to do it instead of falling into a dull, autopilot rut of dissatisfaction. Make sure you have enough fun in your week. I'd write more about this, but it's time for my *Dungeons & Dragons* game!

40

Dream Duty

Be True to Yourself Now

I have decided: I cannot get everything done.
This comforts me greatly.
—*Amanda F. Palmer, musician*

Today's me

The ups and downs of life, both the big and the small, are easier to ride out when you acknowledge that you're made up of many selves with different moods.

> Accept that you are who you are, in the mood you're in today. Recalibrate to that current baseline and try to do the things that today's me does best.

When you define your top few goals, it is often worthwhile to choose two supporting projects for each, which reflect very different skills (for example, "writing the book" and "selling the book" or "planning the new office layout" and "cleaning out the old boxes under the shelf in the back"). This can allow you to move ahead on the most important things in multiple moods.

Not only will your mood and strengths fluctuate from day to day but, over time, most things about you are going to change. No one should expect to keep the same tastes their entire life. Times change and people grow as they are exposed to new ideas, cultures, and subcultures.

- Who are you now? How have you changed since you last asked that question?

- Are you doing projects based on the old you's available time, energy and interests?

- Do these projects still fit you?

Run through your mental list of "I really ought to get better at ..." goals.

- Do they still fit you and the you that you want to be at the end of this year?

- Are your expectations of yourself up to date?

- Is your job still right for you?

If a person doesn't stay the same their whole life, there's no reason to assume that the same work will always be the best fit for them. Skills grow, interests shift, opportunities open up, and needs rise and fall; in other words, *we change*. Our work can change with us; the age of the monoculture career is over. The job that makes you happiest will involve something you love, so do what you can hardly help not doing. Go where your whole-hearted engagement matters.

Be you

Which roles or responsibilities have you perhaps held back from filling based on old notions that no longer match your environment? Discardia takes place on a cultural as well as a personal scale. One of the most exciting examples is how we've moved on as a society from socially and legally mandated gender roles. The pool of available people to fill different roles in civic life has increased, and individuals are better able to match their reality to their true selves. How does this new freedom open up your possibilities?

Let whatever feeds your soul serve its natural purpose, even if that purpose doesn't seem terribly grand or traditional to others.

Keep finding yourself

Ask yourself:

- What do I love?

- With whom do I want to share my time?

- When do I feel most myself?

- How can I pare what surrounds me down to that which is right in this moment?

- What matters to me now?

- Why am I doing anything that doesn't bring me closer to this?

This doesn't mean that everything you do is always fun, but it should serve your goals. Think about your constants. What's been part of your life for 10 years? 20? Longer? How do those things relate to your priorities?

Writing journals is a great way to identify and observe our answers to these questions, and analyze how they change over time. Writer Barbara Ueland praised the value of keeping a free-flowing diary: "It has shown me more and more what I am—what to discard in myself and what to respect and love."

Embrace the knowledge that the shelf life of all plans is limited. The payoff of regularly reviewing your plans is realignment with current reality and goals.

Dream duty

When we re-examine our belongings after self-reflection, we begin to see how letting go is deeply intertwined with being honest with ourselves. Our stuff comes to represent us; comes to be a physical manifestation of our worth as a person. Perhaps worse, it comes to represent the self we dream of being but into which we haven't yet made ourselves.

I call this "dream duty." You might say, "If I don't get rid of this guitar/ skateboard/ ballroom dress, I will eventually get around to using it proficiently, even though I don't practice." Folks, ya gotta fish or cut bait. Start making time to work on that dream or let it go. If you want to fit into those pants again, eat less and exercise, or get a pair like them in your current size.

How do you decide whether to keep the dream or its associated objects in your life? Rather than trying to decide about a particular object, come at it from the other angle: What are your dreams *now*?

Take some time, give yourself permission to imagine anything, and see where your heart leads you. Decide what really matters to you, where you really want to be heading, and then look again at the dream-duty objects taking up space in your home. If those things aren't part of your top goals, get them out of your way.

Again, as with souvenirs, acknowledge who you were when you dreamed those dreams and allow yourself to be someone different now. Sometimes you'll find that your dreams have changed, and that's the easier situation to deal with. The hard one is when you still have the dream but it just doesn't seem realistic. You may still want to be a ballerina but, if you're about to celebrate your 40th birthday, you will probably have to figure out what part of that dream held the most appeal and how you can get *that* without having to trade yourself in for a body 20 or 30 years younger.

What about your dreams is pointing the way to your happiness? Focus on the next step toward your goal rather than the accessories to your initial fantasies of that dream life. If you do this, you'll be moving in the right direction.

Just as acquisition doesn't intrinsically solve problems or improve your life, the props you associate with your dreams don't intrinsically make them come true.

Send away the stale surroundings

Look at the things you've had in front of you for so long that you've stopped seeing them. Do they still match who you are? It's okay to be done with them. Is the artwork on your walls still what you want to see every day? What about that stuff stuck to the front of your fridge or next to the phone? If those knick-knacks on the windowsill aren't you anymore, send them to a new home. Is everything you always have with you still thoroughly you?

If you want to get reinspired for letting go of things around your home, take a break from it. Spend some nights somewhere else—ideally more than four—where you can relax. Before you come home, think about what you actually missed; these are the definite "keeper" things. A good place to start discarding would be the junk for which you walk in and say, "Jeez, I forgot I even *had* that!"

Between these distinct categories, you'll find that time away leaves you in a clearer mental space to distinguish between that which you keep more as the "Museum of Me" and less as something you use and enjoy now. One of the great patterns of Discardia is "fresh eyes," or setting something aside long enough (or clearing your thoughts enough) to view it anew, free from habits that have formed around it. Culture shock is a wonderful teacher of this pattern. Whether you travel abroad, or just stay out of your garage or spare room for a few days, take the opportunity to re-view your home, your work, and yourself.

———

It's hard to move on from old selves and the old stuff that goes with them. One of the most obvious reasons is the comfort of the familiar. Old things are known and nonthreatening. They may not have any relationship to what you want for yourself now or in the future but simply represent the residue of your past choices. You associate old things with situations you've already been through and—apart from getting in your way when you're looking for something else—they do not challenge you. Old things feel safe because they do not represent a risk of failure. You hang onto old stuff that isn't part of who you are now to keep from leaving the familiar nest and flying on new wings.

Go beyond getting rid of items that you don't like anymore, to looking at ones you do like but don't use. Ask, "Can I free myself of this?"

———

While you're letting go of stale dreams, take a good hard look at the skills you tell yourself you're supposed to have. Is that to-be list current?

Stop kicking yourself for not being good at a skill you no longer want to maintain. Priorities shift and that's okay. Outsource that task.

Celebrate all your selves

You may learn that it's also time to diversify your habit portfolio. How do you spend most of your day? Are you building some opposites into your free time to keep yourself balanced? If you're getting where you want to be professionally, your day includes lots of things you enjoy and at which you excel, but that doesn't mean you're necessarily getting all you need.

Stretch out into your full spectrum. Think about your days and about what you might be underemphasizing in your life. For example, if you spend your workday in email, browsers, instant messenger, team meetings, and the occasional presentation to a large group, what's missing? Being outside; not sitting; being away from the web; handling physical objects (other than to-do lists); playing; participating in activities without deadlines; getting mental rest; being aware of your body; creating something completely under your control; reading for pleasure; and writing for pleasure. Find your list of the things that will create balance in your life.

Spend an hour right now doing something to celebrate your whole self. Listen to your heart—and not social norms—when you decide what you most want to do. Let go of trying to conform to someone else's idea of what your taste ought to be. Like what you like! Break out the crayons and color, start up that epic game campaign, practice some skateboard tricks, or launch a kickball league—anything that makes you grin.

Bad guys are optional

As with making room for all of what makes ourselves who we are, loving someone well means making room for each of you to be your best self. Sometimes those selves aren't meant to be together, and that's not always an awful thing. No one has to be the bad guy for each of you to move on to the relationship in which you're meant to be.

Be honest and true to your loves and learn as much as you can from each other. If you don't wind up exploring that long good road together, may you transform the tears of loss over what might have been into happy tears as the guests at each other's weddings when the time comes.

Sometimes the best friends we can have are those who've helped us, even painfully, learn what it is that we really need. As his ex-girlfriend Micki Krimmel, founder and CEO of NeighborGoods, said at the wedding of designer Jonathan Grubb to producer, actress, and cellist Kestrin Pantera of the rightness of their union, "I want to be involved in their whatever, forever."

Love can be bigger than the relationship where it began.

———

Acknowledge your beginnings and accept when you've grown beyond them. Be true to who you've become.

41

Dreamblindness

Awareness Creates Opportunity

> As it turns out, you can say, "Let's make our lives
> awesome!" and the Internet will be like "Oh, it's on."
> —*Maggie Mason, publisher and event creator*

Dream!

Get together with someone you like and respect and talk about your dreams. These are not necessarily those things your brain does while you sleep, I'm referring to the things for which you've been consciously wishing in the past and lately.

What we're longing for and daydreaming about is very important to who we are. It informs the stories we want told about us when we're gone. Talk with someone today about who you've wanted to become, what turned out, and what you're dreaming of now. Maybe you'll also talk about how to make those current dreams real, but that's not the most important thing today. Just talk, remember, and mull things over. Put some ingredients in your mental soup pot and see what it cooks up after you let it simmer for a week or two.

The life list

One fun way to help awaken your sense of what you'd really love to have in your world is to make a list of 100 things you dream of doing. I, like many, was inspired to make a life list by my friend Maggie "Mighty Girl" Mason, and it has paid off beautifully. Getting those wild ideas out of your head and out where you can see them really does help them happen. Relax. Don't try to edify yourself as you make your list. Be bold and happy! Dream as big or as little as you want.

Maggie has your back when it comes to any naysaying that may arise: "You may hear a voice in your head saying that something you want is stupid, or too small, or not interesting enough. The voice may insist that your biggest dream will never happen. Why are you hanging out with that voice? That voice is a total dick."

Writer and photographer Karen Walrond has blogged about creating your life list and offers additional valuable advice: "Under no circumstances should you put something on your list that will make you feel bad about yourself for not completing it. ... Your life list should be about adding moments of joy to your life, not about adding moments of guilt."

Acknowledge the pull you feel toward something, whether it's "more hot baths!" or "visit the Great Rift Valley in East Africa where our species began."

Assessment day

Give yourself an assessment day to compare how are things are currently going versus this time last year.

- What's changed and what hasn't?

- What did you welcome into your life?

- What unpleasantness did you discard?

- What do you still want to change?

- How did you transform your home or your self?

A year is never 100% good, so don't just think about the ups and downs. Give yourself credit for all the little places where you gave your life a nudge toward the life you want to be living. Do a little soul searching. Take a stroll around your house. Balance your checkbook and get a picture of your overall financial situation. Note your progress, your problem areas, and your next steps. When you keep a calm spirit and a clear eye to see things as they really are, you'll be most effective in changing things for the better.

———

This kind of brief stepping back can be valuable when you have the feeling that a whole lot of things suddenly went wrong. As Clay Shirky advised, ask yourself, "What filter just broke? What was I relying on before that stopped functioning the old way?"

Once you do that bit of thinking, it's a lot easier to put your effort into adjusting to make the new circumstances function better rather than merely treating the symptom of a bigger shift.

Moving the big changes forward

What is slowing you down or getting in your way? Draw a bull's-eye on it in your mind and start looking for ways to purge it from your life. What's the first thing you can do to chip away at it or minimize its impact on you? Write that thing down on your planner on the first day where you have a free hour and do it.

To get a better job, update your resume. Deeds are better. Back up your claims and use examples rather than claiming general skills. "Revised plan and achieved successful delivery by 10-person project team when deadline shortened" will sell you more effectively than "Flexible and organized." Once your resume reflects your current strengths you can start searching for an opportunity and spreading the word among friends about what you're seeking.

To get a better place to live, write down your minimum requirements and nice-to-have's. Take a good hard look at your budget and see what you can really afford. Start to save for the first month and security deposit. Weed out stuff you don't want to take to your new place.

To achieve more progress on your side projects, make sure you're set up for success. Pull together your support materials and create an always-ready workspace. Eliminate distractions.

> Start, every day—even if it's only for
> 15 minutes' progress.

Concentrate on a big goal and find one thing that you can do to bring it closer to reality.

Trust yourself

You are already smart. Step back from the noise and listen to yourself. Increased progress toward your goals often comes more from better tools and processes than it does from new data. When you make it a regular habit to take time out, think about your commitments, and organize your ideas, the logical next steps will reveal themselves. When you know what your potential next steps are for each of your projects, it becomes much easier to find one to fit your present context and energy level. When you can easily find something satisfying to do in any given moment that moves you toward one of your goals, you will more rapidly achieve more of your goals.

Align the moment with the big picture

A best practice that can pay off more than any other is to stop trying to keep track of everything in your head. These days we've all signed on for more stimulating input than any one person can fully engage with in a lifetime.

"You receive too much information, and it's not your fault. Just accept that there is more information than time, and that it's increasing every day," said Mark Hurst in his book *Bit Literacy*. The essential trick in the face of this daily onslaught is to think in advance and to respond appropriately in the moment acting in accordance with your priorities. This is as true for a creative professional as it is for someone who works with structured plans in an office.

Comedian and actor Rob Corddry said, "The randomness of my job is one of the most interesting things about it, but that randomness feels less chaotic if I have all of that disparate clutter out of my head and categorized." By learning the tools and techniques to regularly clear your head and review your goals and projects, you free yourself to act on new input in ways that help get you where you want to go.

Distractions are transformed into opportunities or their negative impacts are minimized. "In truth, I've found that any day's routine interruptions and distractions don't much hurt a work in progress and may actually help it in some ways. It is, after all, the dab of grit that seeps into an oyster's shell that makes the pearl, not pearl-making seminars with other oysters," said author Stephen King in his book *On Writing*.

Taking the real stuff of your daily life and using it to produce your best outcomes radically changes your experience of the world for the better. This practical approach to being focused and open to change creates a more balanced life at work—and away from it—and a happier you, even in the face of moment-to-moment chaos.

Define your work in terms of success conditions

Think about whether your job description says, "Have an empty inbox and no loose papers on the desk." I'm guessing that it probably doesn't. Instead, it might have something to do with building customer satisfaction, keeping superiors or clients informed about the status of ongoing work, producing results on those projects on time and under budget, etc.

It's hard to remember, but let go of the illusion that your job will be done properly when you're "all caught up." Dig out the job description and comments from your last review, and see what the real measure of "things going properly" should be. Put it in priority order. Write it up and discuss it with your boss to refine it as necessary. Keep it handy in your day planner or as a text file that you set as the default page in your browser, so you see it every time you open a new tab at work. You want to end up with a touchstone that you can pull out when you feel overwhelmed, adrift, or unrewarded.

This kind of list is crucial for anyone whose work doesn't reach regular cycles of completion and congratulation on a weekly or monthly basis. Stick it up on your wall and refer to it whenever you need to decide what you should work on next.

Here's a sample list for someone maintaining a sales team's software demonstration machine:

- Have investigated and resolved (or have resolution in progress) on all reported problems with demo server
- Have reported status of problems to stakeholders

- Am aware of demonstration schedule (to avoid conducting maintenance during demos)

- Software on demo server up to date

- Server status web page on intranet current with software versions, known issues, and links to demo scripts

- Am aware of upcoming software updates, including new examples that will need to be set up

- Am aware of technical requirements for upcoming updates, and reported shortcomings to manager with a plan for their correction

- Am familiar with products being demonstrated

- Am familiar with operating system and hardware being used, particularly with security and backup needs and techniques

- Am keeping an eye out for ways to improve workflow for self and coworkers

- Am making progress on long-term, nontimebound projects

- Am making progress on professional growth goals

Imagine our hypothetical sales engineer after a wild morning of resolving some surprise software issue which cropped up just before an important demo. He's coming up for air, trying to remember on what he had been planning to work today instead of that crisis du jour that fell in his lap.

He shouldn't start by trying to resolve completely everything represented by each email in his inbox. Instead, he should run down the prioritized list of conditions above and do what needs to be done to achieve that state for each one in order.

He's going to scan his inbox and voicemail for any newly reported or unresolved issues on the demo server that require his action. He's going to make sure that he's let the necessary people know where everything stands now, and of any pending actions and who is doing them. He's going to take a quick look at the demo calendar to see if there's anything new for which he needs to prep.

He's going to check the status on development and see if there is new software coming. If so, he will work around the demo calendar to schedule the next software update, again notifying the necessary people and adding any downtime to the calendar. He's going to look to see if he needs or wants to do any other operating system or server maintenance at the time of that update. He's going to take a quick look over the server status intranet page he maintains and make sure it's current.

Then he can start looking to the nonurgent mail from the development team or listservs that keep him up to date on what's coming in the longer term. He can thus plan accordingly and send out any necessary questions to the developers to help avoid last-minute crises.

Once all these conditions are met, he can broaden his activities to gaining deeper knowledge of his company's products and of the tools he uses or might want to start using. He can also take this knowledge and propose improvements to his own and others' workflow. He may prepare a description of a longer-term project based on these ideas or continue working on an already approved such project.

When all is in order and moving forward properly, he can take time to work on professional growth such as the acquisition of new skills, participation in professional activities like conferences or publications, or other activities that he and his manager have identified as desirable for his continued growth and success.

It is very important to note that he can actually reach the bottom of that list—and be doing his job beautifully—with lots of mail in his inbox and lots of papers on his desk. Those things are not the measure of a job well done. However, they may be very distracting, so one of his priorities for ongoing professional development is to hone his skills at cutting the clutter to help stay focused.

> Create your own high-level, prioritized pictures of "being on top of things" for your work and personal worlds, and then repeatedly check in with them from the top down.

Giving yourself a solid footing from which you decide what you need to do next will make the right things happen for you.

Driving your present choices from your long-term goals

Now back to those dreamy dreams I mentioned at the start of this section. Do the priorities you are currently following reflect them? Just as you repeatedly return to that solid footing when choosing your next actions throughout your day, you should also return weekly, monthly, quarterly and yearly to the increasingly higher levels that represent your projects, goals, values, and vision for yourself.

Let the choices you make about what is important at these higher levels flow down and inform the lower choices. When this is working, you are giving yourself the tools to have your smallest actions serve your deepest dreams. Awareness of your hopes for yourself throughout all levels of the choices you make helps you recognize the most powerful opportunities for you when they arise. If you've already thought about what "better" and "best" look like, you can choose the right response when they knock on your door.

Onward!

The only genuinely subversive thing you can do is
have more fun than other people. So get to it!
—*Bill McKibben, environmentalist and writer*

My Discardian life

As I look back on my life so far with Discardia in it, I find that one of the most valuable habits to start was, surprisingly perhaps, one of the smallest and most simple: Whenever I'm using something—a room in my house, my calendar, or my computer—regularly asking, "What doesn't belong here?" and then doing something about it. This question, along with all the other great deciding moments—Yes or no? Keep or donate? Commit to or move off my list? Finish or cut my losses now?—is at the heart of all the progress I've made.

Why is my home more pleasant than it used to be? It's not that I set out to clean the whole house more often; rather, it's the accumulation of lots and lots of almost unnoticed moments of tidying up, such as carrying an empty glass back to the kitchen, or moving a tchotchke I no longer love into the charity box. It's throwing out that already configured install file sitting on my computer desktop, and clearing the small coins out of my pocket. It's swirling water with my hand around the sink after brushing my teeth to clear away the toothpaste residue, and wiping the top of the stove with a sponge while I wait for something to heat in the microwave.

Why is my head less stressed than it used to be? My world hasn't magically become free of all pressures and aggravations; instead, it's that the worst of them have been optimized against, one small change at a time. Preparation makes me less likely to get knocked off balance. Accounting for possibilities has cushioned me against irritations and enabled me to take advantage of opportunities when they arise. Honesty, with myself and with others, has steered me away from bad habits and negative drama. Knowing who I am, what works for me (and what doesn't), and staying focused on what I love has filled my sails and brought me into ever-happier waters.

The little changes add up.

Keep steadily leaning in the direction of the life you want to be living. As you rid yourself of what doesn't help you, you'll be left with more of what does and your life will be better. You'll have more energy and opportunity to optimize for improvement. Every now and then, you'll stop and notice how much gradual progress you've made without huge efforts. Celebrate this achievement and let it inspire you!

The Discardian community

When you're seeking more inspiration, join with other Discardians online and share your trials and triumphs. The Discardian community is growing every day, and there are hundreds of great stories already out there on the web from which to learn.

In addition to the holiday's home at Discardia.com, you can find it on Twitter as @Discardia (I promise not to overload you with too many messages per day!) and on Facebook at http://facebook.com/discardia. These are the communities I've started. You'll also find Discardia's seeds scattered in blogs, forums, and other publications on and off the web.

Finding time

Do not be deceived into thinking that you can't spare the time to achieve massive changes in your life. You have an enormous surplus available to you if you tap into a tiny fraction of the time of which you currently aren't making positive use. The transformation of your life doesn't have to come from spending all your time doing new things. It can be merely the result of consistently taking 1% of your passive time and making it active.

Where is that passive time? For most people, it's watching TV. In a 2008 lecture, Clay Shirky presented his estimate that the Internet-connected population of the world watches roughly a trillion hours of TV a year. If we took 1% of that time, by his calculations, we could create—in their entirety, including not only the entries but all the web programming and discussion behind them—100 projects the size of Wikipedia per year, at 100 million hours of thought apiece. Small changes add up!

You can find passive time throughout your day. It comes with mindless activities, sure, but it's also during interstitial moments—getting up to get a glass of water, standing in a line, or waiting for someone. These minute opportunities are lying fallow.

One percent. That's all you need to ask of yourself. Just take 1% of your time and effort—even 1% of only your relaxation time—and start using it to make your life better.

Where your time goes is where you're going.

Discardia is an attitude as much as an act

You don't need to make a lot of massive changes all at once or do every activity I suggest in order to be a Discardian. Just commit yourself to change, and consider carefully the new things you bring into your life.

Do what you can. If you don't have time or energy to clean that closet, give it 30 minutes, or go through the things on one shelf or even deal with just one problem object. Too busy when the Discardia holiday rolls around? Take care of yourself, stay focused on your priorities, and celebrate it for a few hours this time instead of the whole season.

Don't burn yourself out doing more than is necessary to reap the benefits. Finish your first rounds of purges before you lock yourself into a new arrangement for things. Don't spend a ton of money on new organizational toys until you're really sure you'll get enough benefit from them. For example, maybe before you buy some expensive storage compartment system, you should dry run the concept with stacked shoeboxes.

Whatever you do, though, do a little something that starts you moving in the direction you want to go. Discard inertia and do one thing—just a little thing—right now.

You deserve a life you love.

Glossary

80/20 rule. A general principle of spending 80% of your time on the 20% most important activities (Symptom #9)

Agile self development. A technique of focusing on a limited list of quickly achievable goals over a limited amount of time (usually between one week and one month) in order to reap benefits faster and be able to adjust more frequently to changing conditions than is possible with larger, longer plans (Symptom #8)

Chunks. Groups of items representing the same kind of action or supporting the same active project; distinct from "stacks," which are amorphous blobs of unknown obligation ("March Discardia: Getting Started")

Completion by deletion. The priority-affirming act of deciding to remove something from our actual and internal to-do lists (Symptom #26)

Dream duty. A quality of belongings which represent an unachieved goal (Symptom #40)

Five-minute fairy. That magical being into which you can sometimes turn without significant effort or even remembering, but which your future self praises highly (Symptom #2)

Fresh eyes. The technique of setting something aside long enough (or clearing your thoughts enough) to view it anew, free from habits that have formed around it (Symptom #40)

Friday Night Look-Back. A quick review of what worked well or poorly in the past week (Symptom #33)

Harmonic intersection. That which appears on both parties in a conflicts' lists of acceptable solutions (Symptom #32)

The Lap. Though it takes many forms, always a short burst of activity that is intentionally limited to a brief period in order to maximize motivation to start (Symptom #2)

The Look-Ahead. Examining the upcoming time (and often the equivalent past time) to identify preparations that will reduce or avoid hassles (Symptom #24)

The man with the hammer. The role to which a creator must shift when it is time to stop tweaking and get the finished creation out into the world (Symptom #6)

Microbreak. A brief respite from focused work, usually only a few minutes, to clear the mind and refresh the spirits (Symptom #10)

Most Important Things. Leo Babauta's technique of choosing a small number (usually three) of priority-driven tasks on which to focus on at a time (Symptom #9)

The Museum of Me. All that we retain which represents who we used to be (Symptom #12)

Nanobreak. The shortest possible break—sometimes only a second—to jumpstart mood and energy with a random encouraging image (Symptom #10)

One Bag at a Time. A decluttering game in which the goal—one less grocery bag's worth of unwanted junk in your life—can be very quickly achieved for a quick win (Symptom #3)

Outbound trains. Receptacles for things that should leave your home—trash, recycling, donations, etc.—and that you always want to have ready to receive more passengers (Symptom #1)

Precuperate. The act of preparing in advance to make yourself more relaxed after future activities (Symptom #24)

Procrastaproductivity. Technique of getting many less important things done while avoiding the big, scary thing at the top of your to-do list (Symptom #6)

Scenario planning. Preparation technique for expected outcomes as well as other possible conditions (Symptom #34)

Shiny Buckets. A way of envisioning the emotional commitments of our priorities as a physical load and monitoring if we are overloading ourselves (Symptom #9)

Stupid simple filing. Putting almost all of the papers you keep in one short stack which you cull when it gets too tall (Symptom #17)

Three Core Principles of Discardia. Decide and Do, Quality over Quantity, and Perpetual Upgrade ("Three Core Principles")

Three-Column Briefing. A quick sketch technique to identify the What, Why, and How of tasks to be done (Symptom #23)

Resources

43 Things. (43things.com).

Adbusters. Buy Nothing Day. (adbusters.org/campaigns/bnd).

Allen, David. *Making It All Work: Winning at the Game of Work and the Business of Life*. New York: Viking, 2008.

____. *Getting Things Done: The Art of Stress-Free Productivity*. New York: Penguin, 2010.

American Psychological Association. "Holiday Stress." 1 December 2006. (apa.org/news/press/releases/2006/12/holiday-stress.aspx).

Amster-Burton, Matthew. "Get Rid of Useless Crap." mintlife. 9 December 2009. (mint.com/blog/saving/get-rid-of-useless-crap).

Anders, Charlie Jane. Writers With Drinks. (writerswithdrinks.com).

Arrington, Jessi. Lucky So and So. (luckysoandso.com).

Athill, Diana. "Why I Love Living in a Retirement Home." *The Telegraph*. 21 August 2010. (telegraph.co.uk/lifestyle/7956692/Why-I-love-living-in-a-retirement-home.html).

Babauta, Leo. *The Power of Less: The Fine Art of Limiting Yourself to the Essential*. New York: Hyperion, 2009.

Baxter, Cinda. The 3/50 Project. (the350project.net/home.html).

Beck, Martha. *The Joy Diet: 10 Daily Practices for a Happier Life*. New York: Crown, 2003.

Blanke, Gail. *Throw out Fifty Things: Clear the Clutter, Find Your Life*. New York: Springboard, 2010.

Blogger. (blogger.com).

Bonner, Sean. "Technomads Presentation for Ignite Toronto 4." Technomads. September 2010. (thetechnomads.net/post/1058694304/heres-the-slides-from-the-presentation-sean-gave).

Brand, Stewart. *How Buildings Learn: What Happens after They're Built.* London: Phoenix Illustrated, 1997.

Cameron, Julia. *The Right to Write: An Invitation and Initiation into the Writing Life.* New York: Jeremy P. Tarcher/Putnam, 1999.

Carlomagno, Mary. *Give It Up: My Year of Learning to Live Better with Less.* New York: William Morrow, 2006.

Carlson, Richard. *Don't Sweat the Small Stuff at Work: Simple Ways to Minimize Stress and Conflict While Bringing out the Best in Yourself and Others.* New York: Hyperion, 1998.

_____. *Don't Sweat the Small Stuff—and It's All Small Stuff: Simple Ways to Keep the Little Things from Taking over Your Life.* New York: MJF, 2007.

Carroll, Jon. "Tiger, Tiger, Not so Bright." SFGate. *San Francisco Chronicle.* 11 December 2009. (sfgate.com/cgi-bin/article.cgi?f=/c/a/2009/12/11/DDTV1B1R4T.DTL).

Carter, Jimmy. "Losing My Religion for Equality." The Age. 15 July 2009. (theage.com.au/opinion/losing-my-religion-for-equality-20090714-dkov.html).

Carver, Courtney. Project 333 | Experiments in Living with Less. (theproject333.com/getting-started).

_____. "7 Ways Dressing with Less will Improve Your Life" BlogHer. 25 May 2011. (blogher.com/7-ways-dressing-less-will-improve-your-life).

CatalogChoice. (catalogchoice.org).

Children of Hoarders. (childrenofhoarders.com).

Coates, Tom. "Is the pace of Change Really Such a Shock?" Plasticbag. org. 26 April 2006. (plasticbag.org/archives/2006/04/is_the_pace_of_change_really_such_a_shock).

Coulton, Jonathan. "I Crush Everything." 12 March 2008. (youtube.com/watch?v=4bBFfMhZLmA).

_____. "I'm Your Moon" 22 May 2009. (youtube.com/watch?v=PcsSTcXMolw).

craigslist. (craigslist.org).

DanKam: Colorblind Fix. (itunes.apple.com/us/app/dankam-colorblind-fix/id406739331?mt=8).

Dansky, Jeri. "Tip of the Month: Decluttering as a Treasure Hunt." Professional Organizer. 24 January 2011. (jdorganizer.com/2011-01-organizing-tips.html).

Digh, Patti. *Life Is a Verb: 37 Days to Wake Up, Be Mindful, and Live Intentionally*. Guilford, CT: Skirt, 2008.

Dillard, Annie. *The Writing Life*. New York: HarperPerennial, 1990.

Doland, Erin. "Tips for returning to normal after a large disruption." Unclutterer: Daily Tips on How to Organize Your Home and Office. 22 March 2011. (unclutterer.com/2011/03/22/tips-for-returning-to-normal-after-a-large-disruption).

——. "How to break up with stuff after a breakup." Unclutterer. 25 March 2011. (unclutterer.com/2011/03/25/ask-unclutterer-how-to-break-up-with-stuff-after-a-break-up).

Earnest, LJ. "Filing Heresy: One Box Filing." SimpleProductivityBlog. 21 January 2009. (simpleproductivityblog.com/filing-heresy-one-box-filing).

eBay. (ebay.com).

EpicWin. (rexbox.co.uk/epicwin).

Flickr. (flickr.com).

Frank, Ze. "The Earth Sandwich." Ze's Page. May 2006. (zefrank.com/sandwich).

Frauenfelder, Mark. "The Nitty-gritty of Whittling down Your Possessions." Boing Boing. 17 August 2008. (boingboing.net/2010/08/17/the-nitty-gritty-of.html).

Friedlob, Cynthia. The Thoughtful Consumer. (thethoughtfulconsumer.blogspot.com/).

——. *How to Get Dressed Without Driving Yourself Crazy*. Kindle/Amazon Digital Services, 2011.

Frost, Randy O., and Gail Steketee. *Stuff: Compulsive Hoarding and the Meaning of Things*. Boston: Mariner, 2011.

Gaiter, Dorothy J., and John Brecher. "Savoring a Storied Evening: The Many Ways to Celebrate Open That Bottle Night; Sediment and Sentiment." *The Wall Street Journal*. 27 January 2006. (online.wsj. com/article/SB113831595267457543.html).

Gawande, Atul. "Letting Go: What Should Medicine Do When It Can't Save Your Life?" *The New Yorker*. 2 August 2010. (newyorker. com/reporting/2010/08/02/100802fa_fact_gawande).

Gilovich, Thomas. *How We Know What Isn't So: The Fallibility of Human Reason in Everyday Life*. New York: Free Press, 2008.

Glei, Jocelyn K. "The Cure for Creative Blocks? Leave Your Desk." The 99%. 28 June 2010. (the99percent.com/tips/6650/the-cure-for-creative-blocks-leave-your-desk).

Gmail. (gmail.com).

Goodwill Industries International, Inc. (goodwill.org).

Grady, David. "The Conference Call." 1 August 2010. (youtube.com/watch?v=zbJAJEtNUX0).

Haughey, Matt. "I Lose Something Every Time I Travel." A Whole Lotta Nothing. 14 March 2006. (a.wholelottanothing.org/2006/03/i-lose-something-every-time-i-travel.html).

Havrilesky, Heather. "How hoarding shows cured my hoarding." Salon. 10 April 2010. (salon.com/entertainment/tv/heather_havrilesky/2010/04/10/am_i_a_hoarder/index.html).

Health Month, the game. (healthmonth.com).

Henry, Helga. "Discardia Is upon Us Again." Work to Your Heart's Content. 2011. (helgahenry.com/discardia-is-upon-us-again).

Hipcast. (hipcast.com).

Holmes, Linda. "The Sad, Beautiful Fact That We're All Going To Miss Almost Everything." Monkey See, *National Public Radio*. 18 April

2011. (npr.org/blogs/monkeysee/2011/04/19/135508305/the-sad-beautiful-fact-that-were-all-going-to-miss-almost-everything).

Hourihan, Meg. "Using the good stuff." Megnut. 20 June 2006. (megnut.com/2006/06/using-the-good-stuff.html).

Huffington, Arianna. "Sleep." *What Matters Now*. Seth Godin, 14 December 2009. (sethgodin.typepad.com/seths_blog/2009/12/what-matters-now-get-the-free-ebook.html).

Hurst, Mark. *Bit Literacy: Productivity in the Age of Information and E-mail Overload*. New York: Good Experience, 2007.

International OCD Foundation. (OCfoundation.org).

Johnson, Boris. "Like the Pharaohs, We're Getting Buried by Our Own Possessions." *The Telegraph*. 26 July 2009. (telegraph.co.uk/comment/columnists/borisjohnson/5914680/Like-the-Pharaohs-were-getting-buried-by-our-own-possessions.html).

Johnson, Steven. "Yes, People Still Read, but Now It's Social." *The New York Times*. 19 June 2010. (nytimes.com/2010/06/20/business/20unbox.html).

Kaspari, Debby. "Surviving the Storm." Drawing The Motmot: Nature, Art, and Everything. 13 May 2010. (drawingthemotmot.wordpress.com/2010/05/13/surviving-the-storm).

King, Stephen. *On Writing: A Memoir of the Craft*. New York: Scribner, 2010.

Knauss, Greg. "The Back-Logged Life." An Entirely Other Day. 2 May 2006. (eod.com/blog/2006/05/the-backlogged-life).

Ladd, Susan. "A Journey toward Unlearning Racism." *News & Record of Greensboro, North Carolina*. 02 August 2010. (www.news-record.com/content/2010/08/02/article/a_journey_toward_unlearning_racism).

Lanoie, Julie. Downsize Challenge. (downsizechallenge.info).

LeechBlock. (www.proginosko.com/leechblock.html).

Leonard, Annie. The Story of Stuff. (storyofstuff.com).

Lesser, Marc. *Less: Accomplishing More by Doing Less.* Novato, CA: New World Library, 2009.

Lewis, C.S. *The Screwtape Letters.* New York: Macmillan, 1943.

Mann, Merlin. 43 Folders: Time, Attention and Creative Work. (43folders.com).

_____. Inbox Zero. (inboxzero.com).

Marino, Gordon. "Kierkegaard on the Couch." *Opinionator, The New York Times.* 28 October 2009. (opinionator.blogs.nytimes. com/2009/10/28/kierkegaard-on-the-couch).

Marsh, Nigel. "How to Make Work-life Balance Work." TED: Ideas worth spreading. May 2010. (ted.com/talks/nigel_marsh_how_to_make_work_life_balance_work.html).

Mason, Maggie. "Your Mighty Life Lists." Mighty Girl. 30 November 2009. (mightygirl.com/2009/11/30/your-mighty-life-lists).

Matheiken, Sheena. Uniform Project: Year 1. 2009–2010. (theuniformproject.com/year1/).

Maurer, Robert. *One Small Step Can Change Your Life: The Kaizen Way.* New York: Workman, 2004.

McGonigal, Jane. *Reality Is Broken: Why Games Make Us Better and How They Can Change the World.* New York: Penguin, 2011.

_____. "Super Better—or how to turn recovery into a multi-player experience." Avant Game. 25 September 2009. (blog.avantgame. com/2009/09/super-better-or-how-to-turn-recovery.html).

McKean, Erin. "You Don't Have to Be Pretty." A Dress A Day. 20 October 2006. (dressaday.com/2006/10/you-dont-have-to-be-pretty.html).

Mooallem, Jon. "The Self-Storage Self—Storing All the Stuff We Accumulate." *The New York Times.* 2 September 2009. (nytimes. com/2009/09/06/magazine/06self-storage-t.html).

Morford, Mark. "Why Do You Have So Much Junk? Oh Yes You Do. And There Are TV Shows to Prove It. Question Is, What Are You

Gonna Do about It?" SFGate, *San Francisco Chronicle*. 4 November 2005. (sfgate.com/cgi-bin/article.cgi?f=/g/a/2005/11/04/notes110405. DTL).

National Yellow Pages Consumer Choice & Opt Out Site. (yellowpagesoptout.com).

Negroni, Christine. "10 Days in a Carry-On." *The New York Times*. 06 May 2010. (nytimes.com/slideshow/2010/05/06/business/ businessspecial/20100506-pack-ss.html?src=tptw).

NeighborGoods. (neighborgoods.net).

OmniFocus personal task management software for Mac. (omnigroup. com/products/omnifocus/).

Onstad, Chris. "Achewood: Are You a Hoarder?" *Techland. Time*. 17 November 2009. (techland.time.com/2009/11/17/are-you-a-hoarder).

OpenLibrary. (openlibrary.org).

organdonor.gov. (organdonor.gov).

Pomplamoose. (pomplamoose.com).

____. "Always in the Season." 17 December 2009. (youtube.com/ watch?v=Il-OFaFzHQM).

Powazek, Derek. "Goodbye Yellow Brick Road." Just a Thought. 4 February 2006. (powazek.com/2006/02/000563.html).

Prentice, Steven. *Cool Down: Getting Further by Going Slower*. Mississauga, Ont.: J. Wiley & Sons Canada, 2007.

Pressfield, Steven. *The War of Art: Break Through the Blocks and Win Your Inner Creative Battles*. New York: Warner, 2003.

Purdy, Kevin. "Rob Corddry on Getting Things Done as an Actor." LifeHacker. 6 April 2009. (lifehacker.com/5199293/rob-corddry-on-getting-things-done-as-an-actor).

Rafkin, Louise. "Vows: Kestrin Pantera and Jonathan Grubb." *The New York Times*. 9 April 2010. (nytimes.com/2010/04/11/fashion/ weddings/11VOWS.html).

Reardon, Megan. Not Martha. (notmartha.org).

RescueTime. (rescuetime.com).

Reddig, Randy. "Less 365." Ydnar. 13 July 2010. (ydnar.com/2010/07/less-365.html).

Robinson, D. Keith. "Quick Tips For Gamers." How to get things done GTD. 21 May 2005. (to-done.com/2005/05/quick-tips-for-gamers).

———. "Knowing When To Quit." How to get things done GTD. 17 October 2005. (to-done.com/2005/10/knowing-when-to-quit).

Robinson, Sir Ken. "Bring on the Learning Revolution!" TED: Ideas worth spreading. February 2010. (ted.com/talks/sir_ken_robinson_bring_on_the_revolution.html).

Rosenbloom, Stephanie. "But Will It Make You Happy? Consumers Find Ways to Spend Less and Find Happiness." *The New York Times*. 07 August 2010. (nytimes.com/2010/08/08/business/08consume.html).

Rosenwald, Michael S. "The Mess He Made: A Life-long Slob Decides It's Time to Get Organized." *The Washington Post*. 13 June 2010. (washingtonpost.com/wp-dyn/content/article/2010/06/07/AR2010060703807.html?sid=ST2010061104123).

Rubin, Gretchen. *The Happiness Project: Or Why I Spent a Year Trying to Sing in the Morning, Clean My Closets, Fight Right, Read Aristotle, and Generally Have More Fun*. New York: Harper, 2009.

———. "Eleven Myths of De-Cluttering." The Happiness Project—Tips. 11 November 2009. (happiness-project.com/happiness_project/2009/11/eleven-myths-of-decluttering.html).

St. James Elaine. *Living the Simple Life: A Guide to Scaling Down and Enjoying More*. New York: Hyperion, 1998.

Sanders, Dinah. Discardia. (discardia.com).

———. (facebook.com/discardia).

———. (twitter.com/discardia).

Sanders, Dinah, and Marcy Swenson. Agile Self Development. (agileselfdevelopment.com).

Sanderson, Katharine. "Why It Hurts to Sell Your Stuff." *Nature News*. Nature Publishing Group. 11 June 2008. (nature.com/ news/2008/080611/full/news.2008.886.html).

Science Daily staff. "The More Secure You Feel, the Less You Value Your Stuff." *Science Daily*. 3 March 2011. (sciencedaily.com/ releases/2011/03/110303111615.htm).

Setty, Rajesh. "Enrichment." *What Matters Now*. Seth Godin, 14 December 2009. (sethgodin.typepad.com/seths_blog/2009/12/ what-matters-now-get-the-free-ebook.html).

Seward, Zachary M., and Albert Sun. "The Top 50 Gawker Media Passwords." Digits. *The Wall Street Journal*. 13 December 2010. (blogs. wsj.com/digits/2010/12/13/the-top-50-gawker-media-passwords).

Sher, Barbara, and Annie Gottlieb. *Wishcraft: How to Get What You Really Want*. New York: Ballantine, 2009.

Shirky, Clay. "It's Not Information Overload. It's Filter Failure." Web 2.0 Expo NY. 19 September 2008. (blip.tv/web2expo/ web-2-0-expo-ny-clay-shirky-shirky-com-it-s-not-information- overload-it-s-filter-failure-1283699).

_____. *Cognitive Surplus: How Technology Makes Consumers into Collaborators*. New York: Penguin, 2011.

Six Items or Less: The Experiment. (sixitemsorless.com/the- experiment).

Smallin, Donna. *One-Minute Tips Unclutter Your Mind: 500 Tips for Focusing on What's Important*. North Adams, MA: Storey Publishing, 2006.

Smidlein, Will. TEDx Detroit 2010. September 2010. (youtube.com/ watch?v=JnilHliEIyM).

Smith, Julien. "How to Get Smarter, Sleep More, and Get More Sex— Today." In Over Your Head. 15 December 2010. (inoveryourhead.net/ sleep-is-awesome/).

Smooth, Jay. "How To Tell People They Sound Racist." Ill Doctrine. 21 July 2008. (illdoctrine.com/2008/07/how_to_tell_people_they_sound.html).

Sterling, Bruce. "The Last Viridian Note." The Viridian Design Movement. 18 November 2008. (viridiandesign.org/2008/11/last-viridian-note.html).

Stout, Hilary. "Saying No, No, No Instead of Ho-Ho-Ho." *The New York Times.* 23 Dec. 2009. (nytimes.com/2009/12/24/fashion/24xmas.html).

Sugar. "Dear Sugar: The Rumpus Advice Column #64: Tiny Beautiful Things." The Rumpus.net. 10 February 2011. (therumpus.net/2011/02/dear-sugar-the-rumpus-advice-column-64).

Susanka, Sarah. *The Not So Big Life: Making Room for What Really Matters.* New York: Random House, 2007.

Styn, John Halcyon. "Spreading Warmth." Life Student. 9 January 2011. (lifestudent.com/hub/2011/01/09/spreading-warmth).

Swap.com. (swap.com).

Tang, Jeffrey. "The Clean-Slate Guide to Simplicity." zenhabits. 9 July 2010. (zenhabits.net/clean-slate).

Thorn, Jesse, and Adam Lisagor. Put This On. (putthison.com).

Thunderbird. (mozilla.org/thunderbird).

Trapani, Gina. *Upgrade Your Life: The Lifehacker Guide to Working Smarter, Faster, Better.* Indianapolis: Wiley, 2008.

TurboTax. (turbotax.intuit.com).

TypePad. (typepad.com).

Ueland, Brenda. *If You Want to Write: A Book about Art, Independence and Spirit.* Blacksburg, VA: Wilder Publications, 2010.

Vienne, Véronique. *The Art of Growing Up: Simple Ways to Be Yourself at Last.* New York: Clarkson Potter, 2000.

Walrond, Karen. "On Creating a Life list." Chookooloonks. 27 April 2010. (www.chookooloonks.com/blog/2010/4/27/on-creating-a-life-list.html).

Warren, T.R. *White Hat Leadership: How to Maximize Personal and Employee Productivity*. Layton, UT: Gibbs Smith, 2007.

WikiHow. (wikihow.com).

Wilkinson, Donna. *The Only 127 Things You Need: A Guide to Life's Essentials*. New York: Jeremy P. Tarcher/Penguin, 2008.

Wolchover, Natalie. "Busting the 8-Hour Sleep Myth: Why You Should Wake Up in the Night." LiveScience. 16 February 2011. (livescience.com/12891-natural-sleep.html).

Gratitude

I would like to thank my wonderful partner Joe for being awesome. Also, my mother Jinx for existence and for encouraging me to be a writer. Thank you to: my editor Joanne Shwed; cover model Modesty B. Catt; cover photographer Reverend Dan Catt; cover designer B.J. West; cataloger Rice Majors; literary agents Janet Rosen and Ted Weinstein, whose early advice helped shape the project; many inspiring indie authors; the makers of the tools that helped me build this book: Scrivener, OmniFocus, and "Getting Things Done"; my encouraging friends and family; the musicians whose creations kept me in forward motion; everyone I've quoted and cited in the book; all the Discardians past present and future; and my patient and helpful beta readers/cheerleading squad Jinx, Joe, Rose, Holly, Bryan, Rebecca, Robert, Elizabeth, Heather, Lucia, B.J., Beverly, Jill, Keely, Gordon, Ann Larie, Vicky, Beth, M-D, Anne, Chris, Charlie, Annalee, Sacha, Fred, Jason, and Tara.

CPSIA information can be obtained at www.ICGtesting.com
Printed in the USA
LVOW04s1439100315

429950LV00001B/154/P